How to Succeed *at* University

How to Succeed *at* University

An Essential Guide to Academic Skills and Personal Development

Bob Smale and Julie Fowlie

Los Angeles | London | New Delhi
Singapore | Washington DC

First published 2009

Reprinted 2009

SAGE Publications Ltd
1 Oliver's Yard
55 City Road
London EC1Y 1SP

SAGE Publications Inc.
2455 Teller Road
Thousand Oaks, California 91320

SAGE Publications India Pvt Ltd
B 1/I 1 Mohan Cooperative Industrial Area
Mathura Road
New Delhi 110 044

SAGE Publications Asia-Pacific Pte Ltd
33 Pekin Street #02-01
Far East Square
Singapore 048763

Library of Congress Control Number: 2008932440

British Library Cataloguing in Publication data

A catalogue record for this book is available from the British Library

ISBN 971-1-4129-4716-9
ISBN 971-1-4129-4717-6 (pbk)

Typeset by C&M Digitals (P) Ltd, Chennai, India
Printed and bound in Great Britain by TJ International Ltd, Padstow, Cornwall
Printed on paper from sustainable resources

Mixed Sources
Product group from well-managed forests and other controlled sources
www.fsc.org Cert no. SGS-COC-2482
© 1996 Forest Stewardship Council
FSC

Contents

Biographical details

Bob Smale is a Senior Lecturer at University of Brighton Business School where he has been closely involved in developing the Professional and Academic Skills Programme with Julie Fowlie. His teaching includes aspects of organisational behaviour, human resource management and employee relations, and he also has research interests in employee relations and pedagogy. Bob has a background in the banking industry and employee relations. He was formerly a part-time professional musician and is also a qualified aromatherapist. He has worked in further, adult and higher education for over two decades, as well as delivering personal skills training, mostly in the public and voluntary sectors.

Julie Fowlie is a Senior Lecturer at University of Brighton Business School, where she has been closely involved in developing the Professional and Academic Skills Programme with Bob Smale. Her teaching includes aspects of management, organisational behaviour and human resource management. She has research interests in emotional intelligence and pedagogy. Julie previously worked in the finance industry in a senior management position also having had experience as a bond dealer. She is also a qualified swimming coach and lifeguard. Julie has taught in further, adult and higher education and runs her own training business, most recently designing and delivering a management development programme for a private sector organisation.

Acknowledgements

We recognise that first developing a taught skills programme and then writing a skills book is not so much a work of invention, but rather involves bringing disparate ideas into an integrated, understandable and cohesive format. We have tried to acknowledge in the text the source of particular ideas, but we also recognise that some are in the public domain and are ultimately unattributable. However, we would like to take this opportunity to thank all those who have contributed to this area and from whom we have learnt so much.

In terms of the development of this book we would like first to thank Patrick Brindle, our Commissioning Editor at Sage Publications, for his sound advice and encouragement. Secondly we must also pay tribute to our retired colleague, Professor Tom Bourner, who was responsible for research and publication within Brighton Business School and so kindly offered comment and encouragement, well beyond his formal retirement from the School. Thirdly, we also wish to thank Professor Aidan Berry, Head of Brighton Business School, specifically for his support and encouragement for our project. Fourthly, we must thank Ralph Timberlake for reading and commenting upon the first draft. However, all errors and omissions remain our own responsibility.

We must also pay tribute to all our colleagues, past and present, who have supported and defended an undergraduate skills development programme at Brighton Business School both before and during our tenure – in particular: Sue Ridley, Marian Whittaker, Sian Eggert, Sue Will, Linda Walker, Jela Webb, Tracey Taylor and Midgie Thompson.

Finally, we need to thank our students, from whom we have not only learnt so much, but also upon whom we have tested and developed our ideas.

Introduction

Overview

- Why do you need to upgrade your skills to succeed at university?
- Why do you need to read this book?

Why do you need to upgrade your skills to succeed at university?

This book has been written to help you to develop the personal, academic and job search skills you will need to succeed in higher education, in employment or whatever else lies ahead. Complete the short self-scoring test below to assess your own level of confidence in relation to developing the skills you will need to complete your course successfully.

Activity: Why do you need to read this book?	
You need to self score each question on a scale from 0 to 10, where 0 is low and 10 is high.	
1. How confident do you feel about starting your course and meeting new people?	
2. How much thought have you given to planning your future development?	
3. How organised do you feel you are in terms of your studies?	

(Continued)

(Continued)

4. How good are you at living independently?	
5. How good are you at completing assignments?	
6. How much do you know about conducting research?	
7. How good are you at taking examinations?	
8. How confident do you feel that you can complete your course?	
9. How confident are you about getting a job after your course?	
10. How confident are you about developing your career after university?	
Total score	

Interpretation

What did you score?

- Less than 50%   You will definitely find a lot of help in this book.
- 50%–75%   There is still plenty to learn in this book.
- 75%–100%   You are very confident – read on to confirm your understanding!

Why do you need to read this book?

This book is primarily intended for new undergraduate students in higher education. However, it will also be useful to established undergraduates and to post graduates. We do not seek to be dogmatic but rather aim to provide ideas and inspiration, and to encourage you to think for yourself about what you need to develop. We provide a framework for you to reflect upon and set your own goals and to develop your own path in order to achieve them.

Our experience is that some students underachieve – both in their academic work and in their long-term employability – because they lack some of the basic personal, academic and job search skills. There are clearly winners and losers in higher education, so our question to you is: '**Why should you be one of the underachievers?**'

Much of our work in recent years has been to help students develop their skills, not only in skills modules but also throughout their studies. This book reflects our commitment to you the student, our desire to share our ideas and to help you develop your skills while in higher education and beyond.

Producing good academic work is largely about understanding certain conventions that operate. Imagine trying to play football or tennis if no one ever told you the rules. We do not believe that the processes of learning and assessment should be a guessing game and part of our aim is to demystify the process for you.

However, success in higher education is not all about academic skills. In order to achieve you need good personal skills too. It is no good writing a brilliant essay if you miss the hand-in date and score zero per cent or, indeed, working hard at your revision and then dry up in the exam hall. So issues such as time management and handling stress are important, together with a wide range of other skills.

For most of you, the long-term goal of higher education will be to improve your employability. Many academic and personal skills are what we call *transferable skills*, which means these will stand you in good stead both when looking for employment and in your future careers. There are some particular job search skills that we really want to share with you, skills that can give you an edge in the competitive job market and help you to get the right job.

The book follows the logic of our teaching and is highly interactive. Short sections of narrative are interspersed with activities providing many opportunities for reflection and action. The book contains a number of pedagogic features, which are perhaps best presented by the standard chapter layout and include:

- **Overview** – bullet points outline the content of each chapter.

- **Diagnostic tests** – a short skill set questionnaire/activity is provided for you to assess your own needs in relation to the content of each chapter. These are self-scoring and limited to ten questions.

- **Introduction** – short narrative explaining the content and why it might be important to the successful student.

- **Activities and narrative** – activities are interspersed with sections of narrative. The activities are designed to help link the ideas introduced in the narrative sections to your particular needs.

- **Experience boxes** – these relate real students', lecturers' and in some cases other people's experiences to illustrate points.

- **Follow-up activities** – these include checklists of skill development activities to follow up on.

- **Further reading and websites to look up** – these are provided for further exploration of the subject area.

- **Review and reflection** – these provide spaces for you to log reflections on each chapter in response to some trigger questions.

We are committed to helping students succeed in higher education and beyond, but it's up to you how you use the book. You can work through the book systematically, chapter by chapter, or dip in here and there to support your development – perhaps using the diagnostic tests at the start of each chapter to help identify your needs. However you use the book, we wish you every success with your studies and your life beyond. It is our sincere hope that this book helps you in your journey.

PART 1   HOW TO DEVELOP YOUR PERSONAL SKILLS

1 How to Prepare Yourself for Higher Education

Overview – what's in this chapter?

- Why do you need to upgrade your personal skills?
- Handling the transition into higher education
- Recognising your own motivation to learn, grow and develop
- Understanding your emotions in the developmental process
- Self-efficacy and self-confidence
- Follow-up activities, further reading and websites to look up
- Time for review and reflection

Why do you need to upgrade your personal skills?

Try completing this short self-scoring test, to assess your own level of confidence in relation to developing your own personal skills in order to complete your course successfully.

Activity: Why do you need to read this chapter?	
You need to self score each question on a scale from 0 to 10, where 0 is low and 10 is high.	
1. How confident do you feel about starting your course?	
2. How confident do you feel about meeting new people?	
3. How organised do you feel you are in terms of your studies?	

(Continued)

(Continued)

4. How confident do you feel about your study skills?	
5. How motivated do you feel about completing your course?	
6. How confident do you feel about overcoming any barriers?	
7. How able are you to handle the emotional side of your course?	
8. How clearly can you visualise your next role after your course?	
9. How well do you think you present yourself to other people?	
10. How confident do you feel that you can complete your course?	
Total score	

Interpretation

What did you score?

- Less than 50%   You definitely will find a lot of help in this chapter.
- 50%–75%   There is still plenty to learn in this chapter.
- 75%–100%   You are very confident – read on to confirm your understanding.

What do you want to achieve by studying in higher education?

What do you want to achieve by studying in higher education? This is a question that you may already be asking. Understanding your answer will have a lot to do with you successfully completing your course.

There is a considerable drop out rate during the first year for most undergraduate courses, which is a tragedy for all those concerned. After all the new students had worked hard, got good grades, got there and yet failed at the first hurdle. Why does this happen? More importantly, why should you let it happen to you?

This chapter is first about helping you make a successful transition into higher education. How was your induction? You may have felt confused or overloaded by the end of day one. Then there are the problems of meeting new people and getting your studies organised.

The chapter next considers your motivation – what you hope to achieve and why. What barriers there are to be overcome and how will you do this. How anxious are you about the process? The chapter then goes on to look at how you can handle your emotions in what is a developmental process.

Next, the chapter looks at *self-efficacy* and how you can build self-confidence in order to succeed in your studies, in employment and in all that lies ahead. You might think that this is rather too soon and that perhaps it should be at the end of the book – but read on, it's what it's all about!

Finally there are some follow-on activities, suggested further reading, websites to look up, and some space for review and reflection. Reflection will be a recurring theme of this book. It is simply about thinking – but in a structured way – in order to help us learn, grow and develop.

Handling the transition into higher education

How did you feel on the first day?

The first day in higher education can be quite traumatic for many new students. There will almost certainly be an induction programme organised for you and it could last for a whole week or even for two. Many people feel that they are subject to *information overload* as a series of well meaning 'talking heads' supply endless information – all of which, they tell you, is absolutely essential.

Activity: How did you feel at the start?

1. Write a paragraph expressing how you felt on the first day in higher education.

2. Write another paragraph about how you felt at the end of the first week. Was it better or worse?

(Continued)

(Continued)

> 3.   Write a paragraph about how you felt at the end of the first month. You might need to make a diary date to do this.

What is culture shock?

Culture shock is experienced when people are first exposed to a new and alien culture. They may feel confused and disorientated. When people enter higher education there is always an element of culture shock, because virtually everyone was somewhere else with a different culture before they arrived. International students are often more prone to suffering from culture shock, not only because of differences in the education system, but also because of language and cultural differences. Indeed it is generally true to say that the greater the difference between where you came from and where you are now, the more likely you are to feel the effects of culture shock.

There are good and bad ways to help overcome culture shock. Consider the following two lists.

Good ways ...	**Bad ways ...**
Become more socially integrated (see next section).	Avoid everybody, especially from your course.
Eat in the refectory.	Eat in your room.
Visit the Students Union and see what is on offer.	Cut classes.
Join student societies, attend meetings and activities.	Don't do any work.
Read and file away all that 'stuff' from induction.	Deny what is really happening.
Get your studies organised, check out your timetable, etc.	Resort to drink or drugs.
Log onto the computer system and check student websites, blogs, etc.	Drop out.
Visit the library and check out the facilities and the nearest book shop.	Go home for good!

Activity: Overcoming culture shock

1. Have a look through the 'good ways' outlined above and make a list of things that you need to do over the first few days and weeks.
2. Keep the list in a place where you can see it and tick off things as you achieve them. It's important to record your successes!

Do you feel homesick or like dropping out?

Culture shock can lead to homesickness, and you may feel like packing up and going home. It's very common to feel like this, particularly if you feel overwhelmed by the workload, the place or the people – perhaps all three!

Dropping out of your course is a big decision. It is life changing and so deserves thorough consideration. Knowing *why* you want to leave or stay will be really important if you are going to make the right decision for you.

Activity: Thinking of leaving your course?

1. Try making two lists to consider your reasons for going or staying.

Reasons for going...		Reasons for staying...	
•		•	
•		•	
•		•	
•		•	
•		•	
•		•	
•		•	
•		•	

2. Now consider:
- Are your reasons more emotional or rational?

(Continued)

(Continued)

- Are any of your reasons short term and likely to change?

- What help and support could you access? (See next section.)

Here are some more things you really should do before dropping out:

- Talk it over with your friends / other people on the course. You may be surprised at how much they want you to stay.

- Talk it over with your course leader, personal tutor or any other member of the academic staff you feel comfortable talking to.

- You may have accommodation problems or just be unhappy where you are. There should be an accommodation officer or department you can talk to about this.

- You may have special needs that can be accommodated by the institution and there should be someone to talk to about this, probably a whole department called 'student services' to check out.

- You may actually feel depressed or be suffering from anxiety problems. This is not a reason for leaving, but rather a reason for staying and working through your problems. You should be able to get support through a student counsellor who will probably be accessed through your student services department or student medical centre.

- Your students union can also help with welfare and academic problems and will be experienced in giving advice and support.

Finally, if you have worked through the two lists in the previous activity and accessed the support you need, you will know if you are making a rational or emotional decision to leave. It's very easy to make a snap decision and then regret it. While it may be harder to stay and work through your reasons in the short term, it will be more rewarding in the long term.

A student told us…

One student told us that, having arrived from one of the remotest corners of the world, she found she had no friends and felt nothing in common with anyone in her halls or on her course. She was so homesick that she just wanted to get on a plane and go back home. We encouraged her to hang in and join some student societies in order to meet more people. By the end of the first year she felt sufficiently confident that she didn't even go home for the summer vacation.

How are you with meeting new people?

Meeting new people tends to happen quite naturally for most people in the first few days at university, but maybe you found it difficult or met the wrong people, or maybe it has all gone a bit quiet now. This could be an area that you need to work on in order to integrate and settle in happily at your university or college.

The first time you meet someone is very important. First impressions really do count. People can sense intuitively in the first thirty seconds of an encounter what basic impression they will have of the other person after fifteen minutes – or half a year. For instance, when people watch just thirty-second snatches of staff giving a lecture, they can assess each teacher's proficiency with about eighty per cent accuracy (Ambady, 1993). Almost the same level of accuracy has been found from brief observations in forty-four other studies, including one of people's interactions with bosses, peers and subordinates (Ambady and Rosenthal, 1992).

Activity: Meeting new people

Take a few minutes to reflect upon the following questions:

- Who was the first person you met on your first day?

- What were your first impressions?

Some people find it particularly difficult to talk to strangers and will tend to avoid making new connections. This is known as a *social phobia*, but it can be overcome with perseverance. See also Chapter 4 on handling stress and developing relaxation techniques.

Here are some 'golden rules' for overcoming a fear of talking to new people:

- You have a perfect right to speak to strangers.

- It doesn't matter what they think of you, because you are still you.

- It doesn't matter how many rejections you get because eventually you will get into meaningful dialogue with someone.

- The more you do it, the better it will go and the more your fears will reduce.

- You are OK!

Not believing in the last of these 'golden rules' – you are OK – underpins our fears and phobias. If you can't truly believe it, try pretending that you are OK, acting a role, when you speak to someone. You may be surprised how quickly you begin to believe it! See also Chapter 3 on understanding the role of emotions – transactional analysis.

Activity: Overcoming social phobias

1. Put yourself in a social situation such as a common room at lunch time or student union bar in the evening. Avoid one that is so loud you can't talk or so quiet that you are feeling self-conscious.
2. Think about what you will say to open a conversation. Open questions such as 'how is it going?' are a good start (see also Chapter 3 on questioning and listening skills).
3. Look out for someone who looks friendly and is also on their own.
4. Try out your opening question and try to back this up with friendly questions, exploring what they told you and then perhaps sharing something of your experience.
5. Make sure you keep doing this until you get into a meaningful conversation.
6. Review how it went and try again another time – soon. Avoidance breeds more anxiety, so it's better to keep at it.

How well focused are you on other people?

You can improve the quality of the conversations you have with other people. Three critical factors are: energy, openness and mind focus. These largely determine the presence we can muster and maintain in any given interaction.

Activity: Presence assessment

1. Ask yourself the following questions to measure your current ability to offer others your full presence:

   - On a scale of 1 to 10 (with 10 indicating a mind homing in like a laser beam of pure attention and 1 being a state of total mind-meandering), what is **your focus level** right now?
   - On a scale of 1 to 10, what is your level of **open-mindedness and open heartedness** at this very moment towards other people?
   - On a scale of 1 to 10, what is your energy level right now, in terms of the reserves of **mental and physical vitality and vigour** you can bring to the moment?

2. Now consider how you can use these techniques:

   - You can perform the above simple self-awareness exercise at any time, mentally calculating your score in order to gauge your current level of presence.
   - Consider using it just prior to an interaction with others, initially to prepare yourself emotionally, then midway through an interaction to increase your mindfulness and alertness, and finally as you leave an interaction to assess your overall presence throughout.
   - Used with regularity, the assessment becomes a self-correcting mechanism. Conscious attention to self-awareness can increase your ability to get on with other people.

Orientating yourself to your studies

What is your attitude to work and study? How do you approach study? Although you may be new to higher education, you will know how you were at school or college.

Activity: How were you at school or college?

Did you:	Tick
attend classes regularly?	
participate enthusiastically when you were there?	
do all the work that was set?	
read to support the work in class?	
file your notes away neatly?	
revise thoroughly for exams?	

Whatever you did before, it's now time to get organised for higher education. The emphasis will be much more on independent study, so being organised will be much more important – and if you don't get organised it is going to get very tough.

Contact time with staff may be much more limited in higher education than you were used to in school or college. The emphasis will probably be much more on you becoming an **independent learner**. Therefore knowing what you are supposed to be doing, when and where, and how to access the support facilities that you need, will become much more important.

Here are some ideas to consider:

- **Check your timetable** – sounds obvious, but you need to be in the right place at the right time. Not everything runs to timetable, so make sure you have a system for remembering what you should be doing such as a diary, personal organiser or mobile phone.

- **Full participation** – again it sounds obvious, but it's essential. It's usually true that failure rates correlate very closely to poor attendance patterns. You don't have to be especially gifted to pass, but you do need to turn up and to participate when you get there. Be there in mind and body!

- **Pre- and post-session work** – try to look upon pre- and post-session work as essential parts of the course and not as a nuisance or a 'bolt on'. Actual taught sessions in higher education tend to be relatively short, so post-session work will help to reinforce and extend what you have started to learn in a session and pre-session work or 'prep' will help you understand the next one.

- **IT facilities, library and bookshops** – get logged onto the computer system as soon as you can in order to access online information. Finding your way around the library and checking out the bookshops are all useful things to do in your first few days and will really help you when the pressure builds up later.

- **Notes / folders** – how are you with paper work? If it's all in a messy heap in the corner, it will be a serious setback to your studies. So the first few days is a good time to buy some files and start to learn to love filing! Taught programmes go by very quickly, with new material to take on board every week. Filing things away is good for revision as it helps to refresh your memory about what you studied. In addition it's all there waiting for you when you need material in order to complete assessments.

Activity: Getting organised for study

1. Make a list of things you think you need to do over the next few days and weeks.
2. Keep the list in a place where you can see it and tick off things as you achieve or complete them. It's important to record your success!

Recognising your own motivation to learn, grow and develop

Motivation is simply about motive, for example why go to work? Why study? Why get up at all? It is clear that people do not all have the same motivations, but each of us has to find what motivates us in order to complete a course, get a job or whatever. The questions are: what is going to motivate you to succeed in your course, then in finding a job and in life as a whole?

Try completing the activity box below in order to find out what is going to motivate you and why, what the barriers to your achievement are and what new skills you might need to learn.

Activity: Understanding your own motivation

Write down your thoughts concerning the following:

1. What do you want to achieve during your time at university?

2. Why do you want to achieve this?

3. What barriers do you think you might encounter in achieving your aims?

(Continued)

(Continued)

---

4. What new skills do you think that you will need to learn in order to overcome these barriers?

5. How anxious are you about your ability to achieve your aims? You can score your level of anxiety from 0 (low) to 10 (high) – please circle:

0	1	2	3	4	5	6	7	8	9	10

Identifying what you want to achieve and why at the start of your course is important, because there will always be days when you wonder what you are doing it all for. Many people also feel seriously anxious about their ability to complete their studies. If you are considering dropping out, and many students do, remembering why you are studying and your motivation to achieve can pull you through on dark days.

Activity: Comparing your motivation to succeed

1. Get someone else to complete the questions in the previous activity and then compare your answers. You might want to consider:

    - Are your answers the same or similar?
    - Do you think that they should be so?

2. Note down any differences which you feel are important.

Succeeding in higher education will require you holding onto your dream. Here are a few things you might want to try out:

- Try visualising yourself in a future time, perhaps at graduation or starting a new job. Paint the picture in your mind and put yourself clearly in it (there is more on visualisation in Chapter 2, Visualising your success).

- Try using affirmations. An affirmation is something we say to ourselves because we need to say it. It is a lie until we don't need to say it anymore. It normally starts with 'I', so your affirmation could be as simple as 'I know that I can succeed in my course'. Try repeating affirmations every day until they become redundant. You'll know when that is!

- Try putting your affirmations on notes and put them up in your room to remind yourself what you are doing and why. This can seem quite daft when you are starting your course in the heady days of September or October, but by the dark days of November or February, they could be your salvation.

- Similarly, try putting up pictures or carrying them with you. Many people find friends, family or partners are an inspiration, or maybe it could be a car or a house you aspire to own. If you want to live in another part of the world, try carrying a picture of that place around with you to remind you of your dream.

A student told us ...

One student told us that his ambition was to be an accountant, but clearly this relied upon him completing his course successfully. He imagined himself in his new life, driving a black BMW. To remind himself, he put a picture of one from a magazine over the desk in his room.

Understanding your emotions in the developmental process

The science of moods

One of the biggest and perhaps least talked about factors in your development will be your ability to understand and work with your own emotions and those of others. At the core of this is the idea that, as human beings, we are 'hard wired' to respond to the behaviour and subsequent emotional reactions of other people. One person transmits signals that can alter hormone levels, cardiovascular functions, sleep rhythms and even immune functions inside the body of another. In all aspects of social life, our physiologies intermingle.

In recent years a science of emotion has developed which is known as **emotional intelligence**. This has been defined as:

The ability to express emotion, assimilate emotion in thought, understand and reason with emotion and regulate emotion in self and others. (Mayer and Salovey, 1990)

and as:

The capacity for understanding our own feelings and those of others, for motivating others and ourselves whilst using leadership, empathy and integrity. (Goleman, 1998: 82)

Why are our emotions a potential threat to our success?

Negative emotions can get in the way of our succeeding, not only in our studies but also in employment and life generally. When we are taken over by negative emotions, this is referred to as an **amygdala takeover**. This can be defined as an inappropriate and uncontrolled emotional response. It has four components:

- A trigger, which is a catalyst that stimulates because it generates an impulse.

- A strong emotion that is felt, such as anger, desire or frustration.

- An instant, impulsive, irrational or uncontrolled reaction that is usually inappropriate.

- A subsequent feeling of regret, after the feelings have passed.

When are we at risk of amygdala takeovers?

Predisposing factors	Triggers	Responses
• Tiredness	• Frustration	• Shouting
• Build-up of stress – 'the last straw'	• Value conflicts	• Crying
	• Personal criticism	• Shutting down
• Lots of effort into something	• Unfairness	• Swearing
	• Aggressive behaviour from others	• Physical violence
• Alcohol		

Activity: Amygdala takeover

Think about an amygdala takeover you have experienced.

1. What triggered it?

2. What was your response (that you regretted)?

3. Can you identify anything that made you predisposed to a takeover?

Regions of the Human Brain

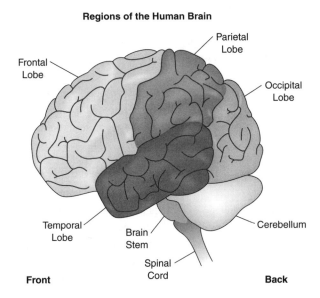

Figure 1.1 Regions of the human brain

Source: http://www.science.ca/images/Brain_Witelson.jpg

Emotions involve an orchestration of activity in circuits throughout the brain, particularly the frontal lobe, which houses the brain's executive facilities (such as planning); the amygdala, which is particularly active during the experience of negative emotions such as fear; and the hippocampus, which adjusts actions to context (Davidson quoted in Goleman, 2003: 186–7).

What are emotional intelligence competencies?

Goleman (2001) has conducted research into competencies which can be observed when an individual is considered to be emotionally intelligent. He went on to develop the competencies framework in the next activity.

Activity: Understanding your emotional intelligence competencies

1. Review the four lists of emotional intelligence competencies ticking those you feel competent in. You are competent in a cluster, when you can tick the majority in the box.

Self (personal competence)	Other (social competence)
Self-awareness Understand own strengths, weaknesses, needs and drives Recognise how feelings affect self Openness to feedback for development Self-confidence based on real strengths	**Self-management** Manage feelings and impulses Choose words carefully Avoid hasty judgements Behave in accordance with values Follow through on promises Open to new ideas and adaptable in the face of new situations Motivate self to achieve Take action to make the most of opportunities in the future
Social awareness Listen to others Understand others' perspectives Sense how others are feeling Understand how the organisation works Committed to helping others (e.g. Patients / Clients)	**Relationship management** Are skilled at winning people over Listen well, seek mutual understanding and welcome sharing of information fully Foster open communication and stay receptive to bad news as well as good Handle difficult people and tense situations with diplomacy and tact Lead by example Model the change expected of others Balance a focus on task with attention to relationships Collaborate, sharing plans, information and resources

2. Review the four lists of emotional intelligence competencies again, this time identifying your strengths and weaknesses, opportunities and threats, and record your findings in the 'SWOT Analysis' below.

What do you see as your strengths in terms of the emotional intelligence competencies?	What do you see as your weaknesses or areas for development in terms of the emotional intelligence competencies?
What opportunities do you see to develop your emotional intelligence competencies?	What threats do you see to you developing your emotional intelligence competencies, or barriers that may need to be overcome?

Self-efficacy and self-confidence

Self-efficacy is about our confidence in our ability to succeed, whether it is in higher education, employment or life generally. Spencer and Spencer (1993: 80) offer a more detailed definition of self-confidence:

> Self-confidence is a person's belief in his or her own ability to accomplish a task. This includes the person expressing confidence in dealing with increasingly challenging circumstances, in reaching decisions or forming opinions, and in handling failure constructively.

Activity: Recognising your success competencies

Spencer and Spencer (1993: 336) have also identified the following competencies that predict success at work and in life:

- **Achievement orientation** – the desire to attain standards of excellence and do better, improve performance.
- **Initiative** – acting to attain goals and solve problems before being forced to by events.
- **Information seeking** – digging deeper for information.
- **Conceptual thinking** – making sense of data and using algorithms to solve problems.
- **Interpersonal understanding** – hearing the motives and feelings of diverse others.
- **Self-confidence** – a person's belief in his or her own efficacy, or ability to achieve goals.
- **Impact and influence** – a person's ability to persuade others to his or her viewpoint.
- **Collaborativeness** – working effectively with others to achieve common goals.

(Continued)

(Continued)

1. Review the above list of success competencies, ticking those you feel competent in.
2. Add your findings to the SWOT analysis you made in the previous section.

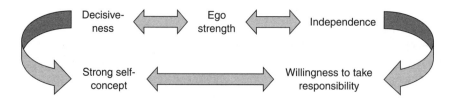

Figure 1.2   Self-confidence – self-perpetuating cycle

Source: Adapted from Spencer and Spencer, 1993: p 81

Spencer and Spencer (1993) state that self-confidence is a component of most models of superior performers, although they also state that self-confidence may or may not be an independent variable: 'Is someone successful because they have self-confidence, or do they have self-confidence because they are successful?'. Both may be the case in a positive self-perpetuating cycle, as illustrated in Figure 1.2

Building your self-confidence will mean doing new things and developing new skills. Whenever we step into new territory we are likely to feel anxious, but we develop confidence by keeping at it and pushing through. Your decision to enter higher education will inevitably mean doing new, different and sometimes difficult things, but the rewards will come from achieving them and from the increased self-confidence that you can take into employment and life.

Activity: Developing your self-confidence

1. Reviewing your SWOT analysis, think of something you could do to build your self-confidence. It may be something you would normally avoid doing or something you have been putting off.
2. Make a definite plan to do something different in your life and then activate it.
3. How did it go? Make a note of what happened.

Follow-up activities

It is quite common in the first couple of weeks of a course not to have much academic work to do, so this may be a good time to invest some effort in what will be important for you over your time in higher education.

TIME FOR ACTION – CHECKLIST

Have you:

- made good efforts to get socially integrated?
- checked out your academic timetable and located rooms?
- started dealing with the information overload by setting up files etc?
- checked out the library and bookshop?
- logged onto the IT facilities?
- accessed any other support services that you will need?
- considered your motivation and how it compares to that of a friend?
- recognised the role of your own emotions and self-efficacy in your development and success?

Further reading

Burns, T. and Sinfield, S. (2008) *Essential Study Skills: The Complete Guide to Success at University,* 2nd edition. London: Sage.

Cottrell, S. (2008) *The Study Skills Handbook,* 3rd edition. Basingtoke: Palgrave Macmillan.

Feldman, R. (2000) *Power Learning, Strategies for Success in College and Life.* Maidenhead: McGraw-Hill Higher Education.

Goleman, D. (2003) *Destructive Emotions and How We Can Overcome Them.* London: Bloomsbury.

Jeffers, S. (1991) *Feel the Fear and Do it Anyway.* London: Arrow.

Lee-Davies, L. (2007) *Developing Work and Study Skills.* London: Thomson.

Pedler, M. and Boydell, J. (1999) *Managing Yourself.* London: Lemos and Crane.

Race, P. (1995) *Who Learns Wins.* London: Penguin.

Race, P. (2007) *How to Get a Good Degree: Making the Most of your Time at University.* Buckingham: Open University Press.

Websites to look up

- Most universities and colleges of higher education will have pages on their own website with titles such as 'arriving at university', 'accommodation', 'dealing with homesickness', 'culture shock', etc.

- The National Union of Students also provides information at:

http://www.nusonline.co.uk/info/freshers/

- Information for international students is available from:

UKISA at: http://www.ukcisa.org.uk/

Time for review and reflection

This is your space to log your reflections on this chapter, to think about what you have learnt, how you will use it and what else you need to find out.

There will be more on reflection and why and how we can use it to learn, grow and develop in Chapter 2, in the sections on recognising strengths and planning personal development.

What were the key learning points of this chapter?
What are your strengths in the areas covered by this chapter?
What areas did you identify for development?
What have you learnt about yourself?
How will you use it?
What else do you need to learn or find out about in relation to this chapter?

2 How to Plan Your Personal Development

Overview – what's in this chapter?

- Why do you need to plan your personal development?
- Recognising your own strengths and areas for development
- Planning your continuing personal development
- Visualising your success
- Overcoming resistance to change
- Reviewing your progress and updating your plans
- Follow-up activities, further reading and websites to look up
- Time for review and reflection

Why do you need to plan your personal development?

Try completing this short self-scoring test, to assess your own level of confidence in relation to planning your own personal development.

Activity: Why do you need to read this chapter?	
You need to self score each question on a scale from 0 to 10, where 0 is low and 10 is high.	
1. How much thought have you given to planning your future development?	
2. To what extent have you decided upon clear targets you want to achieve?	
3. How clearly can you specify your plans or state your targets?	

(Continued)

(Continued)

4. How committed are you to turning your plan into reality and to achieving your targets?	
5. How convinced are you that your plans can become a reality?	
6. How much effort have you put into achieving your targets so far?	
7. How likely are you to resist the process of change?	
8. How likely are you to let obstacles deter you from achieving your targets?	
9. How clearly can you visualise yourself achieving your targets successfully?	
10. Have you set a clear timescale to achieve your goal or dates to review your plans?	
Total score	

Interpretation

What did you score?

- Less than 50%   You will definitely find a lot of help in this chapter.
- 50%–75%   There is still plenty to learn in this chapter.
- 75%–100%   You are very confident – read on to confirm your understanding.

We all need to change in order to grow and develop. Some of this process happens spontaneously; for example you might make a friend who can teach you a new skill such as using a computer package or who helps you to get a vacation job. It's usually good to take up the opportunities which life hands to you, but there is a lot of chance involved in this and it's important to recognise that the process can also be planned. You have a much better chance of achieving what you want if you approach the process systematically.

As a student you might have some fairly obvious targets. Typically our students tell us that they want to have a good time at university, get a good degree and good job at the end. However, what you want out of university doesn't just happen by accident – it's far more likely to happen if you can take on board what we are saying in this chapter.

Personal development planning mirrors the processes of **professional development planning** and **continuing professional development** (CPD) programmes in the workplace. The whole concept of continuing professional development reflects the idea that an initial qualification such as a first degree or professional qualification is not enough and that, in a changing world, updating our knowledge and skill competencies is essential in order to remain a competent professional.

In answer to the question, 'why would people want to change?' Boyatzis (2001; in Cherniss and Goleman, 2001) suggests:

- To increase personal effectiveness or promotion potential.

- To become a better person.

- To help others develop.

Boyatzis goes on to identify four **discontinuities** in the change process, which are those periods when our consistent behaviour suddenly changes, perhaps surprising others and ourselves. The four discontinuities, which can be seen as steps, are:

1. **Deciding who am I and what I want to be** – i.e. real self and ideal self.

2. **The balance between preservation and adaptation**. It may be better to focus upon our strengths rather than our deficiencies, and to decide what we want to keep and build upon.

3. **The decision to change** – the move from contemplation to preparation, making choices and creating your own learning agenda.

4. **The decision to act** – may include a period of experimentation and receiving feedback from other people including friends, family, tutors, etc.

Change may have repercussions when 'they' don't understand. They may be your friends, peers, families and tutors; in a work context they might be bosses, colleagues, subordinates. However, resistance to change may also be internal, as we may fear the process and resist doing what we need to do to grow and develop (see also the section in this chapter on overcoming our resistance to change).

Ultimately, if we are not changing, growing and developing we are likely to start contracting. The status quo is rarely an option because trying to stand still in a changing world tends to lead to our being left behind. This chapter is therefore designed to help you facilitate the process of change and is based upon what we have learned from others and through our own experience of our personal journeys. We invite you to join us!

Activity: What were your targets and what was your motivation?

1. Can you remember what your targets for university were, which you established in the Understanding your own motivation activity in Chapter 1? If so write them here:

2. If you can't remember what your targets were or didn't complete the activity, have a look back at Chapter 1 and complete the motivation activity.

3. Are these targets still important to you?

4. How are you doing at achieving your targets?

In this chapter we aim to help you identify your own strengths and areas for development, to plan your continuing personal development, visualise your success, overcome resistance to change, review your progress and update your plans. Finally there are some follow-on activities, suggested further reading, websites to look up, and space for review and reflection.

Recognising your own strengths and areas for development

Developing a realistic picture of who you are, is the first step in planning your personal development. In particular, it is important to identify your strengths, your areas for development, and your opportunities for development together with any threats or barriers to achievement. You can also include strengths and weaknesses, opportunities and threats from outside life. Making a personal SWOT analysis, as in the next activity, involves looking at the following areas:

- **Strengths** – knowledge, skills and abilities that you already have and may be able to build on. Remembering your strengths is a good starting point and can make you feel more positive about the process.

- **Weaknesses** – potentially these are areas for development if you can work on them in order to turn them from negatives to positives.

- **Opportunities** – these are your life chances and they are all there to be exploited. Even an area for development can become an opportunity to develop.

- **Threats** – are likely to stop you achieving your targets. What are they? Are there barriers which will need to be overcome?

Activity: Who do you think you are?

1. Try to complete the following SWOT analysis.

What are your strengths that you may build upon?	What are your weaknesses or areas to develop and work on?
What opportunities do you see to develop yourself?	**What threats do you see to your personal development or barriers that may need to be overcome?**

2. What did you learn about yourself in the process?

You will find more activities in Chapter 9 (e.g. What skills do I have to offer?) and in Chapter 10 (e.g. What are my personal qualities?) which will help you to identify your skill set and personal qualities. Doing this sort of preparation can really help to inform your personal development planning and also has the potential to expose new areas for your continued personal development.

Planning your continuing personal development

What is the point of personal development planning (PDP)?

Personal development planning is a process we undertake in order to reflect upon our own learning, performance and/or achievement and to plan for our personal, educational and career development. The objectives for **PDP** are to improve our capacity to understand what and how we are learning and developing; and to review, plan and take responsibility for our own learning and development.

In thinking about our personal development we can draw an analogy with a railway journey from one town to another, passing through various stations. Personal development planning is about planning our personal journey through life, and just like a rail journey it can sometimes seem as if we are on a particular track; however, our journey can include a number of stops along the way. These 'stops' are our **review dates**. Reviews allow you to re-confirm or change your objective. In terms of the analogy, we can stop for a while and reconsider – maybe even change trains if we think we are on the wrong track or simply a bit off course.

We can also recognise the idea of the **off course model** (Jeffers, 1991: 126–8) as in the case of a plane or boat which can be off course for as much as 90 per cent of the journey but keeps returning to its heading or course. Watch someone at the tiller of a small boat or the pilot of a small plane and you quickly see that they are off course for most of the journey and constantly correcting their course in order to return to their planned course.

So personal development is not always a straightforward journey from point A to point B. Our lives often contain many twists and turns. Review just helps us to take stock, see where we are, re-plan and move on again. For example, many students get the 'mid-term blues' and maybe do little work or drop out. So it's vitally important to have clear targets, to record them and review your progress towards them regularly. We need aims if we are to achieve anything, because without them we are literally 'aimless'. So targets give us aims in life and can help to keep us on track.

What do you want to develop?

There is no limit to what you can plan, nor do you need to stick to immediate or academic targets, although they should not be excluded. Typical areas for personal development planning include:

- Study skills and study outcomes such as progression, grades and final awards.

- Job and career aspirations including career path and salary.

- Health and fitness concerns including improving exercise, diet and reducing stress levels.

- Personal targets such as climbing a mountain, playing a sport or musical instrument, seeing the pyramids, forming a relationship or whatever else you want to do.

Many students formulate general targets about their degree or job but just what you consider a 'good degree' or a 'good job' is relative – it depends upon what your aspirations are. Think of the image of the medal podium at the Olympic games. You might typically see one athlete ecstatic because he/she is the best in the world, while another is in despair at 'only' getting silver, and sometimes a third is overjoyed because he/she was a complete outsider who unexpectedly got a bronze when nothing at all was expected. Here we see laid bare people's aspirations when compared with the outcomes they actually achieve.

Activity: What do you want to achieve?

1. Brainstorm ideas for things you might potentially want to achieve in life.
2. Next revisit your list and decide what is really important to you.
3. Put what is left into a priority order which you can use in your PDP.

Making your targets SMART

In order to make your plan really effective you need to set SMART targets, which are:

S = Specific

M = Measurable

A = Achievable

R = Realistic

T = Timed

Example of a SMART goal

- **Objectives: What do I want to learn?** To improve my time management skills.
- **What will I do to achieve this?** Break larger tasks down into smaller tasks, make a 'to do list', set deadlines, give myself rewards when I have completed a task.
- **What resources or support will I need?** Work lists, a diary, books (e.g. Smith, H.W. (1998) *The 10 Natural Laws of Time and Life Management*. Nicholas Brearley Publishing).
- **What will my success criteria be?** All tasks on my to do list either completed or rescheduled each day, no work taken home and two hours per week devoted to my CPD.
- **Target date for review and completion?** Review date: 7 February.

If your targets are not SMART you will be less likely to achieve them, and a common reason for failing to achieve is related to making loose targets such as:

- 'I will get better results next semester'

- 'I will be less nervous about exams'

- 'I will get a good job'

The problem here is deciding what words such as 'better', 'less' and 'good' actually mean. A SMART target for results, if this was realistic and achievable, could be:

'I will get an overall 2.1 next semester'

Making a goal which involves measuring your own performance, such as examination nerves, can be more problematic. You could start by making an assessment of yourself on a scale of 1 to 10 and then setting a realistic point to aim for. If 0 was no anxiety and 10 was high anxiety you might make a goal as follows, if you felt this was realistic and achievable:

'I will reduce my level of examination anxiety from seven to three'

Activity: Making a SMART target

1. Try making a SMART target that you might include in your personal development plan.
2. Now check your target. Is it: specific, measurable, achievable, realistic and timed? If not, try re-working it until you are happy that it is.

Making your personal development plan

In terms of making a successful PDP, we recommend that you adopt a systematic approach which includes the following stages:

- Do your preparation first. Complete your 'Who do you think you are?' SWOT analysis activity (see above) so that you have a clearer view of who you are before you start.

- Think before you write. What are your priorities, what is achievable and what is realistic? You can't do everything, and if you try you are likely – very quickly – to become demotivated.

- Set a realistic number of targets and specify each one clearly. What do you want to achieve? Focusing your energy on a smaller number of targets may well bring you more success.

- Think what you will need to do to achieve each aim. There could potentially be several actions for each objective.

- Identify all the resources you will need to achieve each objective. Again there could be several for each of your objectives.

- Consider carefully how you will measure your success. This is the weakest area of many of the PDPs that we see. For some targets the outcome can be clearly measured, as for example 'Achieve 2.1 degree' or 'save £100 from part-time job for Christmas presents'. For others such as increased confidence or reduced anxiety you will have to create your own scale, as suggested earlier in this section.

- Make sure you fix both specific review dates and clear mechanisms for doing it. It is sometimes quite useful to have a 'meeting with yourself' – and you can make a note in your diary, mobile phone or personal organiser to remind you to do it.

Activity: Making a PDP

1. Try completing a personal development plan, using the following format.

Aims:	Actions:	Resources:	Measurement:	Review and timescale:
What do I want to achieve / learn?	What will I do to achieve this?	What resources / support will I need?	What will my success criteria be?	Date and method of review?

(Continued)

(Continued)

2. Critically review your completed PDP or get a friend to look it over. The key questions are:

- Are your targets really SMART?
- Have you fixed a time and method for review?
- Is it just a plan or are you really going to do it?

Research has shown that individuals who set goals are more likely to see behavioural changes if the goals set are highly specific, appropriately difficult, targeted, and remembered – and where the individual remains highly committed (Leonard, 1996). The more detailed and appropriate the level of difficulty, then the greater the self-directed change and the more this increases the possibility of achieving the goal. Therefore, people who specify their targets are more likely to achieve them and the more clearly they specify them, then the more likely they are to achieve.

Visualising your success

Guided visualisation is a key technique in **Neuro-Linguistic Programming** (or NPL) and involves us changing our **subjective experience** or thoughts. Since our brains record all memories, visualisation enables new memories to be recorded, helping us to overcome past disasters and to look positively at the future. It doesn't change what happened, but rather how we feel about it.

NLP was developed by Bandler and Grinder (1976; 1979, cited in O'Connor and Seymour, 2002: 2) and has become the basis of much work in the area of human communications. There are many branches to NLP, but central concerns include:

- Emotional states and how we might change them.

- Studying patterns or language and behaviours as evidenced in situations.

- Building rapport and trust in interpersonal relations, perhaps by mirroring or matching words or behaviours.

- Setting motivational targets and overcoming barriers to achievement.

- Modelling behaviour – discerning the sequence of ideas or behaviours required to successfully achieve a task.

- Reprogramming subjective experience in order to overcome negative thought patterns, such as phobias, or to allow for successful achievement of targets.

In the following two activities, we first try to put something from our past behind us, before turning our attention to what we want to achieve for the future.

Activity: Putting the past behind us

1. Working individually, recall a bad memory, a past failure or something you didn't manage to succeed at – perhaps something that plays on your mind.
2. Note down how you are feeling emotionally at this very minute, while you are recalling your negative memory.
3. Now working with a partner, close your eyes and ask your partner to slowly talk you through the following steps. You can either nod or say yes when they want you to move on to the next stage, but do not share your thoughts with your partner during the process.

   - Visualise your memory.
   - Put a frame around the picture.
   - Turn off any sounds associated with it.
   - Push it away from you so it's about ten feet away.
   - Paint it onto glass so that it's fragile and brittle.
   - Turn it to black and white.
   - Push it far, far away, until it's in the distance.
   - In your mind, pick up a stone and throw it with perfect accuracy at your picture.
   - Watch the glass shatter and the picture break into a million black and white pieces that then dissolve into dust in space.

4. At the end of your visualisation, write down how you felt emotionally at that moment.

Activity: Visualising your successes

1. Working individually, identify something that you want to achieve.
2. Note down how you are feeling emotionally at this very minute.
3. Now working with a partner, close your eyes and ask your partner to talk you slowly through the following steps. You can either nod or say yes when they want you to move on to the next stage, but do not share your thoughts with your partner during the process.

   - Visualise what you want to achieve.
   - Put yourself in the picture.
   - Add any sound or music you would like.

(Continued)

(Continued)

- Check that you are happy with the picture and make any changes you want.
- Indicate that you are happy with it.
- Now increase the brilliance of the picture.
- Check out how you look, breathe and speak, together with any other impressions.
- What emotions do you feel?
- What physical sensations do you feel?
- What are you saying?
- What kind of person you are?

4. At the end of your visualisation, write down how you are feeling emotionally at that moment.

Visualisation also links well with other techniques such as meditation and autogenic training (see also Chapter 4, Handling stress and developing relaxation techniques), and normally involves picturing and recording how we think things realistically might be. If we build a picture in our mind of how we might handle a difficult situation better, we are more prepared when we meet it, because we have already built some of the psychological structures of the experience. For example, if you fear examinations you can try to visualise yourself being relaxed and confident while taking them.

Overcoming resistance to change

As suggested earlier in this chapter, change may have repercussions when 'they' don't understand. Resistance may be internal or external, in other words it could be other people that stop us moving on, but also it could be ourselves. The root of almost all resistance to change is fear and included in this is the fear of failure – getting it wrong, doing badly and maybe being worse off than you are now.

Personal development is partly about getting unstuck from wherever we are stuck and moving on. However, getting stuck would seem to be part of the human condition and most of us seem to suffer from some level of inertia at points in our lives. When you catch yourself saying 'but I always ...' you could be well and truly stuck!

Inertia gives us some hope of security, but it may be a false hope. It is very easy to get trapped in a **comfort zone** and this, of course, avoids the discomfort of having to take steps outside of it. Your comfort zone may in fact be quite uncomfortable, but staying stuck can seem preferable to taking the steps you need to take in order to move on, grow and develop. Here are some examples of false comfort zones:

- Sticking with a group of 'friends' you don't particularly like or respect because it feels safer than making new ones.

- Avoiding your studies because it seems easier in the short term not to go to class or pick up a book.

- Staying in substandard accommodation where you find it hard to study because it is too much hassle to move.

Getting unstuck takes one thing only: commitment to achieving what you want. Making a personal development plan is a sign of your commitment to your own development and so is reviewing it. Getting into the habit of **planning, acting and reviewing** as an ongoing cycle will allow you to see how you are doing. If you are still stuck when you review, then getting unstuck will have to become a target in itself.

One technique for overcoming your own resistance is to try to think in a way which at first disassociates you from the problem. In the next activity you will see a classic disassociative question, which asks you why you think other people in your situation might resist change. From there it's a short step to ask yourself: what about me then? Why might I be resisting?

Activity: Overcoming resistance to change

1. Try to think why some other people might resist change, if they were in your situation.
2. Might you be doing the same thing? If so, how might this resistance be overcome?
3. Think where you expect external resistance might come from. Who or what might want to keep you stuck – and why?
4. How might this resistance be overcome?

As you start to change, you might face resistance from family, friends and significant others in your life who don't understand what is happening to you. Jeffers (1991: 89–108) devotes a whole chapter to this problem entitled 'When "they" don't want you to grow'. This is a problem that many students report when they return home. While they have changed, back home everybody is going round in the usual circles and it can be surprising and distressing to find that you don't fit in anymore. Worse still to find that they think there is now something wrong with you, as often expressed in terms such as 'huh, is that what they teach you then?'.

It is generally good to explain your plans to those around you and to try to get positive support. In general we are more effective when we have positive people around us who appreciate what we are trying to do. However, if you get only negative feedback from any or all of the people in your immediate circle, then it is time to look for a new **cheering squad**. As Jeffers puts it (1991: 90):

> It is amazingly empowering to have the support of a strong, motivated and inspirational group of people.

Reviewing your progress and updating your plans

According to the old adage, 'the road to hell is paved with good intentions'. Making a plan is all well and good, but it could just be fine words if a plan is all that it is. Your plan needs to be activated and you need to review your progress regularly. As we suggested earlier in this chapter, your personal development can be seen as being like a journey, with stops along the way which provide opportunities for you to review your progress, to confirm or change your plans and to make a new review date.

Review dates are not the same as end dates. We sometimes see students setting a target such as 'Get overall 2.1 this year' with a review date to coincide with the release of results. However, that is at a point where they can no longer influence the result. Let's face it, everyone reviews their progress on results day. What they needed was a *series* of review dates over the course of their studies to make sure they were on track and a *final* review date when results come out.

There are many ways of reviewing your progress. You could have a **meeting with yourself** as suggested earlier, or you might have a friend or colleague to buddy up with for some form of peer review of each other's progress. Your institution should have some form of **personal tutor** scheme, so another option would be to ask your tutor to review your plan with you.

One outcome of every review should be to make a new plan or at least to update the existing one, so that you always have a plan in operation. You must also, of course, fix a new review date. So the process is ongoing – a cycle of reviewing, planning, acting and then reviewing, planning and acting again – so that it becomes a form of habitualised behaviour.

Follow-up activities

TIME FOR ACTION – CHECKLIST

Have you:

- reflected upon your progress to date?
- completed the SWOT analysis in order to see what you have already and what you want to develop?
- identified your targets for development?
- made your targets SMART?
- made a personal development plan?
- visualised what you want to achieve?
- identified what resistance you might face and considered how to overcome it?
- fixed review date(s) and method(s) for review and updating of your plans?

Further reading

Buckingham, M. and Clifton, D. O. (2005) *Now, Discover Your Strengths*. London: Simon & Schuster.

Burns, T. and Sinfield, S. (2008) *Essential Study Skills: The Complete Guide to Success at University*, 2nd edition. London: Sage.

Cameron, S. (2008) *The Business Student's Handbook*, 4th edition. Harlow: Pearson.

Cherniss, C. and Goleman, D. (ed.) (2001) *The Emotionally Intelligent Workplace*. San Francisco: Jossey-Bass.

Cottrell, S. (2003) *Skills for Success: The Personal Development Planning Handbook*. Basingstoke: Palgrave Macmillan.

Cottrell, S. (2003) *The Study Skills Handbook*, 2nd edition. Basingstoke: Palgrave Macmillan.

Feldman, R. (2000) *Power Learning, Strategies for Success in College and Life*. Maidenhead: McGraw-Hill Higher Education.

Goleman, D. (1998) *Working with Emotional Intelligence*. London: Bloomsbury Paperbacks.

Jeffers, S. (1991) *Feel the Fear and Do it Anyway*. London: Arrow.

O'Connor, J. (2002) *The NLP Workbook: A Practical Guide to Achieving the Results you Want*. London: Element.

O'Connor, J. and Seymour, F. (2002) *Introducing NPL: Psychological Skills for Understanding and Influencing People,* 3rd edition. London: Element.

Pedler, M. and Boydell, J. (1999) *Managing Yourself.* London: Lemos and Crane.

Websites to look up

- For help and support with personal / professional development planning:

http://spider.ukc.ac.uk/PDP/sitefiles/Keynote_PDP-sitefiles/index.htm
http://www.uncommon-knowledge.co.uk/personal_development/plan.html
http://www.palgrave.com/skills4study/pdp/about/index.asp

- For help and information with visualisation:

http://www.stress.org.uk/8903/9330.html

Time for review and reflection

This is your space to log your reflections on this chapter, to think about what you have learnt, how you will use it and what else you need to find out.

What were the key learning points of this chapter?
What are your strengths in the areas covered by this chapter?
What areas did you identify for development?

What have you learnt about yourself?

How will you use it?

What else do you need to learn or find out about in relation to this chapter?

3 How to Improve Your People Skills

Overview – what's in this chapter?

- Why do you need to upgrade your people skills?
- Questioning and listening skills
- Preparing for formal interviews
- Understanding the role of emotions
- Recognising non-verbal communications
- Resolving conflict with other people
- Asserting yourself when it is appropriate
- Influencing others
- Giving and receiving feedback
- Follow-up activities, further reading and websites to look up
- Time for review and reflection

Why do you need to upgrade your people skills?

Try completing this short self-scoring test, to assess your own level of confidence in relation to improving your people skills.

Activity: Why do you need to read this chapter?	
You need to self score each question on a scale from 0 to10, where 0 is low and 10 is high.	
1. How good are you at talking to new people?	
2. How good are you at framing questions in order to get people talking?	
3. How good are you at listening to other people?	

4. How good are you at saying clearly what you want to say?	
5. How good are you at handling your emotions?	
6. How aware are you of other people's body language?	
7. How good are you at resolving conflict with other people?	
8. How frequently do you assert yourself in situations with people?	
9. How good are you at influencing people?	
10. How open are you to receiving feedback from others?	
Total score	

Interpretation

What did you score?

- Less than 50%   You will definitely find a lot of help in this chapter.
- 50%–75%   There is still plenty to learn in this chapter.
- 75%–100%   You are very confident – read on to confirm your understanding.

Whatever you want to do or achieve in life will definitely involve working and interacting with other people. Clearly we all have a level of skill in this area, but some of us are better than others. The good news is we can all develop our people skills.

However, it's not just a case of developing our own communication skills, because when dealing with other people we are also *interacting* with them and their reactions may be quite unpredictable. We all have bad days and catching someone you know at the wrong moment may require you to change your approach, even to back off altogether.

We all have to handle a myriad of **interpersonal situations** in life and they include:

- **Formal situations** – such as attending a tutorial or supervision with one of your lecturers, conducting your own research interviews for completion of an academic assignment or a recruitment interview for a job or placement.

- **Informal situations** – can involve meeting new friends, catching up with old ones or 'chatting up' in a night club.

We can all learn and develop a range of key skills in this area, including:

- Improved question formulation.

- Listening and hearing skills.

- Reading body language.

- Understanding the emotional content of interpersonal communications.

- Asserting ourselves.

No one handles every interpersonal situation perfectly, but the skills listed above are ones that we can all keep developing through life. These are **transferable skills**, that is skills learnt in one context which can be used in another. Skills learned here can be developed in social situations and then used to further our studies and careers.

In this chapter we aim to help you to develop your interpersonal skills and abilities in handling relationships. We will focus in particular upon questioning and listening skills, preparing for formal interviews, the role of emotions, non-verbal communications, resolving conflict, asserting yourself and influencing others, together with giving and receiving feedback. Finally there are some follow-on activities, some suggested further reading, websites to look up, and some space for review and reflection.

Questioning and listening skills

Asking better questions

We use questions for a variety of purposes including to get people talking, to find out information, and to give direction and reinforcement to our conversations. However, some questions can be more productive than others. We can distinguish three types of question:

- **Open-ended questions** – these generally produce longer answers and get people talking. They usually start with words such as who, what, when, where, which, why, how or tell me. They demand longer answers, so you get more information by asking less questions and your conversation becomes more productive. The most open question is probably, 'tell me about your life'.

- **Closed or directional questions** – these tend to produce short answers because they can be answered with a simple yes or no. They start with words such as do, did, are, might, if, can, does, have, is, etc. Closed questions do help with direction. For example, you might in a job interview ask, 'will there be any opportunities for further training and development?'. If the answer is 'yes', you can follow this up with an open question. Most often this is the real value of a closed question, in establishing whether an area is worthy of further exploration.

- **Reflective questions** – these ask the other person to expand upon their answer. For example, you might be chatting with a friend who mentions planning a holiday in Greece. There are two possibilities here. You could simply repeat the word 'Greece' with an upturn in your voice to indicate a question. Almost certainly your friend will then go on to tell you more about the trip. Alternatively you can ask a question such as 'can you tell me more about that?'.

Activity: Developing your questioning skills

- Try writing some sample questions of each of the three types listed above.
- Next try dropping them into everyday conversations.
- Reflect upon the results you got. Which questions were most effective and why?

Selecting the right questions comes with experience. People who are nervous frequently ask too many questions in general and too many closed questions in particular. It is just a case of practising your questioning skills, reflecting on how it went and gradually improving your technique.

Listening and hearing

Perhaps one of the most frustrating things that can happen in an interpersonal situation, be it socially or in a formal interview, is when you feel that you are not being listened to. It typically happens something like this: You are asked, 'what are you doing at the moment?'. You answer, 'I am studying engineering at university.' and then they ask you, 'And what are you studying at university?'. Why does this sort of thing happen? Well clearly the interviewer wasn't listening to your answer, and you might ask why. The most likely reason is that he or she was distracted and probably more concerned with thinking about the next question, rather than listening to the one in hand.

Listening is the second great interpersonal skill after question formulation, but listening isn't enough. It may sound completely obvious to say, but we also have to **hear** what is said and that is not the same thing at all.

Imagine you are listening to a band or orchestra at a gig or in a concert hall. You listen to the music, but do you hear it all? You might be interested in what one musician is playing, so you focus in on that performance. You hear it, while listening to the whole. It takes attention and concentration and this is what we need for interpersonal communication. This is what we can call **active listening**.

Active listening involves:

- Being fully engaged or 'switched on' to the situation.

- Not speaking unless you are absolutely sure that the other person has finished what they are saying.

- Maintaining eye contact.

- Displaying open body language.

- Triggering the other person to say more with nods or smiles.

Silence is golden! This old expression is very true, because you often find that people will say much more when you give them space and time. A good rule here is, ask less and listen more!

> ### Activities: Listening and hearing
>
> Here are two activities that will help you to improve your listening and hearing skills:
>
> 1. Working with a friend, take turns to interview each other. The interviewer only asks one open question, and then relies upon nods, smiles and other facial expressions in order to get responses.
> 2. When you are in a social situation try asking someone an open question and then try to refrain from saying anything else for as long as possible, once again triggering the other person with nods, smiles and so on.
>
> Note down how long you managed to make these activities last. With practice you will be able to ask less, but elicit more from people.

Preparing for formal interviews

In preparing for a formal interview, it is important to recognise what type of interview you are planning to conduct. There are three options and each of the following has advantages and disadvantages:

- **Structured interviews** tend to revolve around a preset agenda and scripted questions. They can in one sense be very thorough, because some thought has been put into deciding what needs to be covered and also into formulating the questions. However, these can be very stilted in practice and the formality can intimidate the interviewee. Also the interviewer may miss something really important altogether, because no pre-prepared question covered it.

- **Informal interviews** are often the best because you can be very relaxed and this will encourage the other person to open up and talk. However, they may be quite unsystematic, rambling around from point to point and again may miss some points in the process.

- **Semi-structured interviews** are a compromise and have the advantage of having some structure whilst allowing some flexibility. They allow points to be introduced and then to be explored more fully with supplementary questions.

> ### Activity: Developing interview questions
>
> - Before you conduct an interview, do some preparation by making a *mind map* (see Chapter 5 on mind mapping) in which you identify all the areas you want to explore.
> - Rather than scripting questions in advance, try using your mind map as a crib sheet during the interview. Use closed questions to open up new areas when necessary and then open questions to explore them.
> - Afterwards reflect upon how it went, making a note of what went well, what did not go so well and what you would do differently next time.

When conducting an interview it may be useful to consider adopting the following systematic approach:

- Think in advance what you want to achieve from the interview and what you want to know. Making a mind map – as in the last activity – can often help focus your thoughts.

- Seek a *comfortable* environment in which to conduct the interview – somewhere that both your interviewee and yourself will feel comfortable. It should ideally be clean, tidy, well-ventilated and neither too hot nor too cold. Not being comfortable can be a major distraction from the interview process.

- Try to avoid any interruptions by putting a notice on the door and put the phone on divert. There is nothing worse than somebody crashing in just as you have asked the most difficult question. The moment can be lost forever.

- Organise the furniture and, if possible, sit side by side; face to face is too conflictual. Too far away is too distant and too close is threatening (see also the following section on recognising non-verbal communication).

- Start your interview by making introductions; be welcoming, friendly and use first names to relax your interviewee.

- Always explain the purpose of the interview, stating how long it is likely to take and what is going to happen. Doing this will help to relax and reassure your interviewee.

- Ask your questions giving your interviewee plenty of time to reply, and also giving your interviewee opportunities to ask questions.

- Summarise the interview and explain what will happen next.

Four **golden rules** of interviewing are:

1. Always listen closely to answers.

2. Give time and space.

3. Don't interrogate.

4. Don't be judgemental / prejudiced.

Activity: Developing your interview skills

Working in a group of three, take turns to play the role of:

1. An interviewer working for an employment agency, who is trying to find out as much as possible about the interviewee.
2. A student interviewee seeking work who is unsure as to what work he or she might best be able to do.
3. An observer who will time the activity, take notes and give constructive feedback after the interview, using the following questions:

   - What questions were used (i.e. open, closed, reflective)?
   - How well did the interviewer listen to the answer and was sufficient time given for the interviewee to reply?
   - What body language was displayed?

Understanding the role of emotions

What is Transactional Analysis?

Transactional Analysis was first developed by Berne (1968; 1975) and provides us with an invaluable tool for understanding the emotions which underpin inter-personal communications. However, he also gives us:

- A theory of personality.

- A model of interpersonal communication.

- A method of analysing patterns of behaviour.

More recently Stewart and Joines (1987) have provided a workable textbook on Transactional Analysis and this section, for the most part follows the key concepts they have identified. Try working through them one concept at a time, recording your thoughts in the activity box that follows each one.

The ego state or PAC model

Berne (1968; 1975) argues that emotional responses are encoded in childhood, before the age of five, and stored in three sets: parent, adult and child. As we learn child responses through our experience of childhood, concurrently we learn parental responses from those who brought us up. We all have these emotional responses at our disposal, but some will be more developed in some people than in others.

Our **parent** is our protector, guardian and critic and is divided into controlling or **critical parent** and **nurturing parent**. Today, each is frequently subdivided into positive and negative aspects.

Our **adult** is our rational self, but it is not an ideal state, as we need our parent to warn us and our child for play.

Our **child** is also divided. The **free**, **natural, rebellious** or **glee child** is happy and playful, while the **adapted child** or **depressed child** conforms to rules and societal norms but may be difficult, petulant or irritable. They are also often now subdivided into positive and negative parts.

According to Berne (1968; 1975) all our emotional responses can be categorised under one of these headings. We have all learnt and encoded a range of emotional responses and are constantly **switching** between them. You may easily observe this in yourself and others, when something triggers a **switch**. For example an otherwise calm and rational individual, who normally drives very well, may suddenly react with road rage when triggered by some relatively minor incident.

It may be that one ego state is dominant, and that you may be predominantly drawing upon your critical or nurturing parent, rational self, free or adapted child.

Activity: Ego states

1. Which do you think is your dominant ego state or states?
2. Try to come up with an example of ego state behaviour, drawn from your own experience of life, for your:

   - Critical or controlling parent
   - Nurturing parent
   - Adult
   - Glee child
   - Depressed child

Transactions

The **transaction** is seen as the basic unit of interpersonal communication and all transactions are seen to involve an exchange of communications between two or more individuals. Transactions may be:

- **Complimentary** (lines parallel)

- **Crossed** (lines not parallel)

- **Ulterior** (contains covert message)

Two examples of **complimentary transactions**:

Parent to child: You should be careful with saving that work, you know what happened last time.

The implication is I'm OK and you are not OK.

Child to parent: 'I really don't need you to keep reminding me about saving the work.'

The implication here is you're not OK, I'm OK, but *you* don't realise.

Adult to adult: 'So, how is the work going?'

Adult to adult: 'It's going fine thanks.'

The implication here is I'm OK, you're OK, and we can discuss the work without it being an issue.

An example of a **crossed transaction**:

Boss asks calmly: 'Have you finished the report yet?'

The transaction is ostensibly adult / adult and the implication is, I'm OK / you're OK.

Subordinate replies hysterically: 'Report, report, what do want, blood or something!'

Here the depressed child is responding to a perceived critical parent. The implication is, you're not OK and neither am I.

An example of an **ulterior transaction**:

Boss asks tersely: 'Have you finished that report yet?'

The overt message here is adult to adult, but the covert message is critical parent to child, 'You should have finished it by now' – i.e. you're not OK.

Subordinate asks boss: 'Will everybody be kept on after the merger?'

The overt message is adult to adult but the covert message is depressed child to parent, 'Will I be kept on?' – i.e. I'm not OK.

Strokes, over stroking and stroke deprivation

Strokes in Transactional Analysis are emotional acknowledgments we give to and get from other people rather than physical strokes. These can be either positive or negative, including encouragement and chastisement. Strokes give us feedback and therefore are part of how we know how we are doing.

Activity: Emotional stroking

Here are some examples of positive and negative strokes:

Positive strokes	Negative strokes
You look good today!	You look awful!
You made a really good job of this!	I see you managed that eventually!
That really suits you!	Did you have to wear that?
You always cheer me up!	You always get on my nerves!

Consider the following questions and jot down what you think.

- Do you give out more positive or more negative strokes?

- Do you give out too many or too few strokes?

- How might giving more positive strokes change a relationship you have?

Stroke deprivation is when no one gives you strokes and perhaps tells you how you are doing. Managers who forget to thank and praise their staff should expect a demotivated workforce! **Over stroking** is experienced when people give you so many positive and negative strokes that it leads to confusion.

Your stroking skills will tend to condition the relationships that you have with those around you.

Life script

Life script is the life story which we wrote in childhood and stored away in our subconscious mind, but of which we may now be quite unaware. There are three possibilities:

- If you had a good life you might have developed a **winning script**, in which case you would expect to be a success.

- If you had a nasty life you might have developed a **losing script** and you might expect to be a failure.

- You might have developed something in between, however, called a **non-winning script** in which you might expect life to be just OK.

The question is, are life scripts deterministic? The really important point here is that our scripts do not determine whether or not we are winners or losers, but rather how we feel about what happens to us in life. When interviewed, celebrities will often say either, 'I always knew I would get to the top' or 'I still can't believe its all happened'. In these kinds of statements, they reveal their life scripts.

> ### Activity: Examining your life script
>
> Consider the following questions and jot down what you think:
> - What do you say about your anticipated future life to yourself?
> - What do you say about your anticipated future life to others?
> - Do you need to say anything different to yourself or others and, if so, what?

Remember, what you say about your life chances to yourself and others will tend to expose your life script.

A student told us...

One student said in a moment of despair, 'Why should I achieve anything, when no one in my family ever has before?'.

Discounting, redefining and rackets

Discounting is when we blank out our perception of reality to fit the script. For example someone might tell you, 'I never had a lucky break', but you know he actually passed up every one that came along.

Redefining is when we distort our perception of reality to fit the script. For example someone might say, 'Everything I do always goes wrong', but she can't explain the excellent degree that she got and the top job she now holds.

Rackets are emotional responses that you were permitted to have during childhood in order to get strokes and which get replayed in adult life. For example, if you fell over in the park when you were four years old, you screamed and screamed and then they bought you an ice cream to keep you quiet, think about what you were taught about the world. People who use emotions in adult life to get a payoff may well be drawing on what they learnt in childhood.

Activity: What rackets did you learn?

Consider the following questions and jot down what you think.

- Which emotional responses do you employ in adult life in order to get what you want?
- What happened in childhood which might have led you to learn this response?

Stamps

Stamps are when we experience a racket feeling and store it up rather than expressing it. We bottle up emotions like people sticking stamps on a card to save up for a television licence. One day we may choose to redeem that card, and when we do the 'flood gates' will open and everything will poor out in a tirade. Typically we are likely to say, 'and another thing …'.

Games and payoffs

A **game** in Transactional Analysis is a series of pre-rehearsed transactions being replayed. We all know some games that are neither sports nor fun games, but instead are life games, played to achieve an outcome or **payoff**. A payoff leads to one party gaining at another's expense. In your working life you will certainly meet some people who will play power games with their colleagues. Some examples of games discussed by Berne (1968) include:

- **NIGYSOB** – 'Now I've got you, you son of a bitch' is the classic 'wind-up' game.

- **SWYMD** – 'See what you made me do' is a blaming game that allows one actor to gain protection from further interruption.

- **WHAM** – 'Why does it always happen to me' allows one actor to play the victim role.

- **ITHY** – 'I'm only trying to help you' is where one player seeks psychological advantage over another by providing unwanted support.

When you get drawn into a game, you may feel that you have played it before. The truth is that you probably have, as most games are well known, especially in close relationships found in families and workgroups. However, there are ways to break a game. The first step is to recognise when a game is being played and that you may have unconsciously consented to be an actor in it. There are then a number of options including:

- Refusing to play by saying, 'I don't want to play this game anymore'. You may be surprised by the fact that even those completely unaware of this game concept will understand that you are terminating the game.

- Take on another role within the game by 'switching' ego states.

- Start playing another game. That really confuses them!

Activity: Recognising game playing!

Consider the following questions and jot down what you think.
- Are you aware of ever playing or being drawn into life games?
- If you answered yes, what could you do to break the game?

In general we can perhaps see game playing as a negative activity and ultimately destructive because it undermines our relationships with other human beings. Learning that we don't need to play games is part of recognising our next point, **autonomy**.

Autonomy

Autonomy involves realising our full potential by updating the strategies we adopted as children. We can do what we want, once we realise that we can. This is the really good news that comes out of TA.

Activity: Claiming your birthright – autonomy!

Consider the following questions and jot down what you think.
- How autonomous are you?

- When you don't do what you want, what stops you? It's a tough one to answer, but look out for words like 'should' and 'ought' which are very 'scripty'.

- What do you need to do in order to become more autonomous?

Potential criticisms of TA

Berne (1968, 1975) is sometimes criticised for being 'Post-Freudian' because he considers that personality is formed in childhood, i.e. by nurture rather than by the impact of nature. The latter view is to some extent supported by the more recent recognition of the impact of DNA. There are also the still controversial arguments about the effects of both our life in the womb and of our often traumatic experience of birth. Therefore TA is perhaps at its weakest as a theory of personality development. So what is the point of using Transactional Analysis? We suggest that TA is invaluable for:

- **Self analysis** – to understand ourselves better, to become less the product of deeply internalised past experiences and more autonomous human beings.

- **Interpersonal skills** – to understand and improve our communications with subordinates, peers, superiors, customers etc.; to break unfortunate communication patterns; and to create more harmonious working lives.

Activity: Updating your emotional strategies

Consider the following questions and jot down what you think.

- If you have a negative relationship with somebody in your life, try introducing more positive strokes. Note how the relationship changes over time.
- Listen to your friends; what do they say about their likely successes in relation to examinations, course outcome, careers and life generally? They will almost certainly expose their life script to you very quickly.
- Ask yourself to what extent you are autonomous and to what extent your life script rules you.

Recognising non-verbal communications

A big part of dealing with other people better lies in how we read and react to non-verbal communication. Mehrabian (1971) has claimed that in terms of our understanding of interpersonal communications:

- 7 per cent of meaning is in the words spoken.

- 38 per cent of meaning is paralinguistic, i.e. in the way that the words are said.

- 55 per cent is in facial expression.

What we display to others and how we read other people's non-verbal communications is a language in itself, often referred to simply as body language. We all make extensive use of non-verbal signals or body language in everyday communications and commonly observed signals include:

- Maintaining **eye contact** and **nodding** from time to time shows interest, whereas positively averting the gaze can clearly signal disinterest.

- General **physical proximity**. Closeness or distance may indicate emotional closeness or distance. We tend to get closer to the people we feel closest to. Similarly, we can feel very uncomfortable when people we don't like get too close to us.

- **Leaning forward** in meetings, interviews or in any discussion tends to show interest, while leaning back tends to show disinterest.

- **Pointing** with elbows or knees may indicate interest in the person pointed at and, perhaps, a sexual interest in a social situation.

- **Matching** or **mirroring** each other's body language tends to show agreement, perhaps even with nodding in unison. These are known by salespeople as *buying signals.*

- Signs of **defence** include crossed arms and/or legs; hiding behind desks, books or folders, big glasses, beards, moustaches; or long hair over the face etc.

Non-verbal communications are often seen in clusters which makes them more convincing. For example, if you are interviewing someone who sits behind a desk with arms crossed and looks out of the window rather than at you, then you are probably fairly safe in assuming a high level of disinterest. However, it is easy to misread a signal. For example someone with crossed arms may simply be cold, rather than defensive. Also, there may also be cultural variations, as for example in parts of the Far East, where it is considered rude to look people in the eye. Contrast this with the Western view which sees avoiding eye contact as a sign of dishonesty.

Activity: A fly on the wall!

Try doing this activity when you are alone but in a crowded place. Travel termini are especially useful places to do this and it helps to fill the time when you get delayed.

- Observe the non-verbal communications of the people you can see who are involved in interactions with others.
- Think how much of their communication you can interpret, without necessarily hearing what is said.
- How many ego states (see previous section) can you read, from people's body language?
- Consider how what you observed in this activity might be useful in helping you to deal more effectively with other people in your everyday life.

Understanding something about non-verbal communications also allows us to take some control of situations by signalling more clearly to others what we want to communicate. Non-verbal communication is not just about body language, we can also think about how to signal things to people in other ways, for example when we set up the chairs for an interview or presentation. In the interview case putting chairs in a circle will, potentially, create a friendlier meeting whereas arranging them face to face will be a more conflictual set-up.

Resolving conflict with other people

There are many causes of conflict in the world from full scale wars over borders, ethnic or religious differences, to the more mundane washing-up crisis experienced in many student households. Completing group assignments is also frequently a cause of conflict and you will find that much of the content of this chapter will be helpful in smoothing the path (see also Chapter 5 on completing group assignments successfully). Fortunately, there are many techniques which can be used to resolve conflicts.

Activity: Evaluating methods of conflict resolution

Consider what advantages and disadvantages there might be to the following methods of conflict resolution:

- **Coercion** or **force** – one party forces the other to submit e.g. terrorism.
- **Manipulation** – facts are intentionally distorted or a situation is dramatised by one party.
- **Acquiescence** – one party gives in to the other.
- **Convergence** – ideas are synthesised or parties 'come together'.
- **Democracy** – people vote and the majority view prevails.

(Continued)

(Continued)

- **Compromise / negotiation** – both parties agree to give something to get something.
- **Conciliation** – a third party acts as go between and gets the parties talking.
- **Mediation** – a third party suggests what might happen.
- **Arbitration** – a third party decides what will happen.
- **Avoidance** – parties avoid a resolution and conflict remains.
- **Denial** – the parties pretend there is no problem.

This activity raises the question: is there a best way to resolve conflict? We suggest that there is not, and that different situations require different methods. Clearly avoidance and denial are not in reality methods of conflict resolution.

When there are arguments, knowledge of Transactional Analysis and non-verbal communications (as discussed earlier in this chapter) can be useful, in order to understand first what is going on and secondly how to change it. Some top tips for reducing tension are:

- Lower your voice and speak as quietly as possible. This lowers the overall volume and the other person will normally lower their voice eventually.

- Be on the same level as the other person. Ask the other person to sit if possible and stand up if they won't.

- Ask, 'Can we make another time to discuss this?', in order to allow for a cooling off period and perhaps to gather more information, if this is appropriate.

- Ask the other person, 'Can we discuss this rationally?'. This is an attempt to force them into the adult rational ego state (see the above section on Transactional Analysis and the role of emotions). They may, however, say no and walk off.

- Ask the other person to put the problem in writing to you. This forces the other party to think more about the issue and often marks an end to the affair.

- Use 'we' instead of 'you' and 'I'. Changing the personal pronouns changes the context. For example phases such as 'we seem to have a problem' and 'could we think about a solution?' move the situation from conflict to a joint problem-solving situation.

Conflict is common and sometimes inevitable when dealing with other people, but developing some skills and techniques can help to minimise and hopefully resolve it. In general, it's better to focus upon common ground, possible solutions and positive outcomes.

Asserting yourself when it is appropriate

What is assertiveness and why is it important?

Are you saying what you really want to say? Do you sometimes fear saying what you mean to say or fear the reaction of others?

From our prehistoric ancestors we have retained two basic responses to trouble, namely **fight** and **flight** (see also Chapter 4 on handling stress and developing relaxation techniques):

- **Fight = aggression**, which is evidenced by violent language or behaviours.

- **Flight = avoidance**, in which we avoid and 'bottle up' problems and are diminished in the process.

Both responses lead to unwanted physiological changes in our body chemistry through increased adrenaline, causing short-term and long-term symptoms. The alternative approach is for us to learn to be assertive.

Every incidence of failure to assert requires two players, a manipulator and a 'nice guy'. For example, consider the following scenario:

> You kindly give me a lift to the supermarket every Friday after work, then one week I say, 'Look I am feeling really tired tonight, and also there is something on the television I want to see. If I give you some money and a list, can you get my shopping for me and drop it round later? After all, I am on your way home.'

If you are such a nice guy that you get my shopping for me, have you allowed me to manipulate you? What would be the implication of you refusing to get the shopping?

> **Activity: How assertive am I?**
>
> Assess how assertive you are by taking the following test. Circle the letter for the response that, in your opinion, best answers each of the following questions.
>
> 1. You are in a long line to pay for your lunch. Someone walks up and moves into the line in front of you. The assertive thing to do is:

(Continued)

(Continued)

    a. to complain to others around you in a loud voice.

    b. to ask the person to go to the end of the line.

2. Which of the following is a reason to be assertive?

    a. to achieve your goals.

    b. to show who is right.

3. The definition of assertiveness usually includes the following:

    a. 'deny the rights of others'.

    b. 'ask for what you want'.

4. A non-assertive person may respond to a situation with non-verbal cues such as:

    a. a whiny voice.

    b. direct eye contact.

5. Aggressive words from others violate your right to courtesy and respect. Which of the following is an aggressive comment?

    a. 'Don't be such a fool.'

    b. 'Would you mind very much if we skip the formalities?'

6. Which of the following is an appropriate assertive response?

    a. keeping your opinions to yourself when you are angry with your boss.

    b. asking your boss for a meeting in which you can express your point of view.

The correct answers are: 1: b   2: a   3: b   4: a   5: a   6: b

Learning some assertiveness techniques

Assertiveness techniques help us to express our needs in a way that is polite and generally acceptable to others. Most of the time people are cooperative and thoughtful, but when conflict arises people respond in different ways. Some act aggressively, some passively, and some assertively. In order to become more assertive, here are some techniques that can help:

- Remember that no one can manipulate you, unless you allow him or her to do so.

- Avoid *knee jerk* reactions. In a busy life it is easy to feel that we have to respond to every situation immediately.

- Give yourself thinking time. Take stock and think what you should say or do. It could be nothing!

- Learn to say no, when it is appropriate to do so.

- Learn how to say no, avoiding 'I can't' which is negative and diminishing in favour of 'I won't', which is your positive choice.

- Learn to say yes when you *want* to and not because you think you *ought* to.

- Be persistent when necessary. Smith (1975: 73–87) talks about the **broken record**: 'I won't, no I won't', etc. Eventually they will get the message.

If faced with a threat of violence it may be better not to act assertively, but rather **non-assertively**. If you are being held at knifepoint or a car is speeding towards you, an assertion will be of little use. Flight and/or fight are still appropriate responses in dangerous situations, which is what 'Mother Nature' designed them for.

Activity: How do I know when to be assertive?

1. Smith (1975: 28–71) has given us ten assertiveness rights. Try working through them and tick any that you have difficulty with:

    - You have the right to judge your own behaviour, thoughts and emotions, and to take responsibility for their initiation and consequences yourself.
    - You have the right to offer no excuses to justify your behaviour.
    - You have the right to judge whether you have the responsibility for finding the solutions to other people's problems.
    - You have the right to change your mind.
    - You have the right to make mistakes and to be responsible for them.
    - You have the right to say 'I don't know'.
    - You have the right to be independent of the goodwill of others before coping with them.
    - You have the right to be illogical in making decisions.
    - You have the right to say 'I don't understand'.
    - You have the right to say 'I don't care'.

2. Review the items you ticked in the list.
3. In order to gain ongoing benefit from the work you have done on assertiveness, complete the following tasks:

    - Identify situations where either you did not feel that you asserted yourself or perhaps that you did it in an inappropriate way.
    - Think what you need to do differently in the future.
    - Make a diary date to review your progress after, say, one month.

Influencing others

Achieving your goals (see Chapter 2 on personal development planning) often involves influencing those around you, in order for you to develop and progress. However, people don't like to feel they are being used or manipulated and it is easy to make enemies in the process. The good news is that most people seem to like being helpful, if they are approached in the right way, and so it is important to win people over to your cause. Cooperation will be a key word.

There is no one way to influence people around you, but here are some ideas to work through.

- **Goals** – being clear on your goals and what you want to achieve is a good starting point. Your goals can become a focus for everything else you do. Try practising what you learnt in Chapter 2, reminding yourself regularly of your goals and visualising your success.

- **Interpersonal skills** – improving these involves developing the skills covered in this chapter. This will help you to achieve your goals by improving the interactions you have with others. This development will include your interview skills, understanding emotions, non-verbal communication, and being able to assert yourself when required.

- **Networking** – is an active process in which you commit yourself to building your network of contacts with others. You never know when a contact will become useful, so it is always worth asking for a phone number and giving them yours.

- **Relationship building** – is also an active process, not this time involving casual contacts but rather those who will help and encourage you. In higher education this will include both your friends and friendly tutors. It is good to work out who is going to be important to you and to give them your attention.

- **Leadership** – some situations require you to put yourself out front, for example when completing a group assignment. Someone will have to take the lead and they will most probably have the biggest influence on the final result, so, why not make sure it's you? See also Chapter 5, Completing group assignments successfully.

- **Confidence** – people will be much more likely to react positively to someone who displays confidence in what they are doing. Try to act as if you count, even if you are not sure whether you do. It's amazing how confidence grows when you start to do this and people start to take you seriously. However, avoid arrogance as that will tend to alienate those you need to help you. There is a fine line between confidence and arrogance – and it's very important to recognise it.

Activity: How can I develop the art of persuasion?

Cialdini (2001) suggests that we can harness the 'science of persuasion' as follows.

PRINCIPLE	APPLICATION
Liking: People like those who like them.	Uncover real similarities and offer genuine praise.
Reciprocity: People repay in kind.	Give what you want to receive.
Social proof: People follow the lead of similar others.	Use peer power whenever it's available.
Consistency: People align with their clear commitments.	Make their commitments active, public, and voluntary.
Authority: People defer to experts.	Expose your expertise; do not assume it is self-evident.
Scarcity: People want more of what they can have less of.	Highlight the benefits and exclusive information.

Read through the above table, noting down what you need to do differently in order to become more persuasive.

In terms of influencing and persuading, it is essential to consider how you approach people. It's not just a question of what you say and how you say it, but also to whom, when and where.

Letters tend to get filed or – worse still – binned and emails overlooked or deleted, so face-to-face or telephone communications are always preferable. If you do have to write, make sure you call first to get a name, address and position. If you don't get a reply you can always back this up with a phone call, politely asking if the named recipient received your letter.

A student told us...

A student told us that he had telephoned a major corporation (which will remain nameless) for help with a research project and that they had been very unhelpful. When asked how many people he had spoken to he replied, 'One'. He was then informed that the corporation currently had in the region of 160,000 employees and that he might just have been unlucky. He tried again, and got the help he needed.

When calling an organisation, it is often best to explain who you are and what you want, and then to ask who could help you. It doesn't matter how many times you get transferred, if you get to the right person in the end.

When you are referred from one person to another, try to get the name of the person referring you as well as the person you are passed on to. You can then introduce yourself by saying, 'Mr/Ms X suggested I talk to you'. It helps to break the ice.

If someone works in a busy office, can you set up a time to take him or her for a coffee, in order to sit down quietly and have chat? Alternatively, can you make an appointment to see them?

Activity: Developing your influencing skills

- Consider who you need to influence in order to achieve your goals.
- Consider how you might best approach them, what to say, when and how – i.e. the best way, best time, best place.
- Activate your plans, review how they are going and be prepared to change your approach if it is not working.

Giving and receiving feedback

We all learn about the world through feedback (see Chapter 5, Why is reflection important to learning?) but the quality of feedback we receive, how we receive it and how we use it is highly variable. We all give and receive feedback quite naturally, even without speaking we use body language, including eye contact – or the lack of it! See also the discussion above on recognising non-verbal communications.

Imagine taking a draft of your report or essay – over which you have worked long and hard – to your tutor for some feedback. Which of the following responses would be the most useful:

- Its rubbish!

- It's brilliant!

- You make some very good points here, however there are a couple of other things that you should say which I have noted in the margin. You use a good variety of sources, but I notice that one, which I have underlined, does not trace to your bibliography. The presentation is generally good, but you should start a new page for your bibliography.

The first two examples are highly **subjective** and use what we can call **emotive language**. They actually tell us nothing about what is right or wrong, or indeed good or bad, about the work because they reflect only the emotions of the reader. In contrast the third example appears to give a more **objective** commentary on the work. It also uses the **sandwich technique**, which is often used to deliver the bad news more kindly and within a more objective context.

As a student, you will need to get regular feedback in order to progress. This may come in many forms, but if you find yourself in a feedback vacuum, don't be afraid to ask, 'How am I doing?'.

Much of your feedback may be in written form, in particular when you get assignment work returned to you by your tutors. The next time this happens, notice how many other students just look at the grade and ignore the written comments. To get the most out of your written feedback we suggest that you:

- Read everything carefully, including cover sheets notes on the work and any other documents used, such as assessment grids.

- Ask questions of your tutor if there is anything you don't understand or simply can't read. If he or she is too busy at the time, ask for an appointment.

- Think about what has been written, what you can learn from it and what you might need to do differently in the future.

The feedback we give impacts upon others just as much as the feedback we receive does. You may well also be in the position of giving feedback to others and this might include:

- when working in teams or on group assignments.

- as a mentor to other students as part of a mentoring programme.

- when reviewing another student's work informally or as part of a formal peer assessment programme.

- when completing feedback documentation on your course and / or modules.

There are some clear guidelines for giving feedback effectively (adapted from video material, Davis, 1999) and these include that feedback should be:

- objective rather than subjective or emotive.

- based upon identified criteria. With assignment work, the objectives should be clearly stated in the brief. If they are not, ask your tutor for them, preferably before you start on the work.

- specific rather than generalised, in order to tell you what is actually right and wrong.

- descriptive, so as to provide a useful level of detail. 'Could do better' is not acceptable in this day and age!

- structured, so as to cover everything point by point.

- essential, in that the feedback should stick to what you **need to know** rather than what is merely **nice to know** – in other words, it avoids waffle.

- constructive rather than destructive, because the aim should always be to help you to develop.

- non-evaluative, because giving feedback on your work is not the same as judging you.

With regard to the process:

- Fixing a convenient time and finding a suitable place is important. Being rushed or uncomfortable will naturally detract from the process and for feedback, the **corridor meeting** – although much loved in universities – is not acceptable.

- Feedback can often usefully start by asking the other person how they felt the activity went. Often we are our own sternest critics, and the role of the person giving feedback can then become to put our own thoughts into perspective.

- There should always be time for a two-way discussion and for the person receiving the feedback to ask questions.

- The process should end by making a plan for future action and perhaps making a date to meet again, if this is appropriate.

When we receive feedback we have to be prepared to listen and take it on board. Goleman (1998: 263) suggests that

Feedback can be a priceless tool for self-examination and for cultivating change and growth.

Baddeley (1990) suggests that when we look at a particular situation, we see it through the lens provided by the mental models we have built up through past experience, education or training. We approach situations we encounter with a mindset, a recipe we have acquired from the past, and we use that to understand what is happening and to decide what response/action to take. The mental models we create may or may not be the most appropriate given the situation, or we have not had enough experiences, education or training to develop the most appropriate response to a given situation.

Activity: How good am I at receiving feedback?

This self-assessment will help you measure your current skills in receiving feedback. For each of the statements, tick the 'rarely', 'sometimes', or 'often' box to indicate how consistently you use the described behaviour.

	Rarely	Sometimes	Often
1. I truly listen to what feedback givers are saying.			
2. I keep feedback in perspective and do not overreact.			
3. I try to learn from all feedback, even if it is poorly given.			
4. I am willing to admit to and learn from questions about my performance or behaviour.			
5. Rather than avoiding feedback, I attempt to turn every feedback session into a useful encounter.			
6. I accept redirections, reinforcing rather than denying them.			

(Continued)

(Continued)

7. I accept responsibility for my role in achieving individual, team and organisational goals.			
8. I accept responsibility for searching for solutions to performance and behavioural problems that threaten goals.			
9. I accept responsibility for keeping my emotions in check during feedback discussions.			
10. I am committed to listening and learning from all feedback sessions.			

In general when receiving feedback we suggest that you:

- Listen! It is so easy to go into **private circuits**, especially if you are still thinking about the last point when the next one comes up.

- Try to confirm what has been said by using reflective questions (see the section in this chapter on questioning and listening skills), e.g. 'Could you explain that?' or 'I'm not sure but did you say…?'.

- Take notes, because you won't remember everything that is said.

- Conclude positively, thanking the person for their comments – whether negative or positive, and whether you agree with them or not.

- Consider what has been said and be open-minded. It's all too easy to be defensive about criticism or even praise if you underestimate yourself.

Activity: How am I doing?

- Consider the question: How do I know how well I am doing?
- Review the feedback you have received to date.
- Ask for additional feedback if necessary.
- Consider what all this tells you about how you are doing and what you need to do as a result.

Finally, we ask you to not be afraid to ask for feedback from your tutors, your peers and anyone else who can help. Ensure that you are clear about assessment requirements and don't wait until you get a bad mark before asking for help. Try to be open to the feedback process and learn as you go. Too many students fear the process, especially when they are struggling, and so avoid it and then fail.

Follow-up activities

TIME FOR ACTION – CHECKLIST

Have you:

- practised your interpersonal skills by asking closed, open and reflective questions?
- learnt to recognise both your own emotional responses and those of others?
- considered how you can use your knowledge of non-verbal communications?
- thought about how you might use alternative strategies to resolve conflict?
- asserted yourself when you had the need to do it?
- considered when and where you need to use persuasion techniques?
- asked for feedback on how you are doing?

Further reading

Berne, E. (1968) *The Games People Play*. London: Penguin.

Berne, E. (1975) *What Do You Say After You Say Hello?* London: Corgi.

Cameron, S. (2008) *The Business Student's Handbook*, 4th edition. Harlow: Pearson.

Goleman, D. (2003) *Destructive Emotions and How We Can Overcome Them*. London: Bloomsbury.

Guirdham, M. (2002) *Interpersonal Skills at Work*, 3rd edition. Harlow: Pearson.

Hunsaker, P. L. (2005) *Management – A Skills Approach,* 2nd edition. Upper Saddle River, NJ: Pearson.

Lee-Davies, L. (2007) *Developing Work and Study Skills*. London: Thomson.

Mehrabian, A. (1971) *Silent Messages*. Belmont, CA: Wadsworth.

Moon, J. (1999) *Reflection in Learning and Professional Development*. London: Kogan Page.

Moon, J. (2006) *Learning Journals: A Handbook of Reflective Practice and Professional Development*, 2nd edition. Abingdon: Routledge.

O'Connor, J. (2002) *The NLP Workbook: A Practical Guide to Achieving the Results You Want.* London: Element.

Pease, A. (1984) *Body Language.* London: Sheldon Press.

Russell, T. (1994) *Effective Feedback Skills.* London: Kogan Page.

Smith, M. J. (1975) *When I Say No I feel Guilty.* New York: Bantam.

Stewart, I. and Joines, V. (1987) *TA Today.* Nottingham: Lifespace.

Websites to look up

- For general help with people skills / interpersonal communications:

http://www.ezinearticles.com/?People-Skills:-Eight-Essential-People-Skills&id=12294

- For further information on transactional analysis:

http://www.itaa-net.org/ta/keyideas.htm
http://www.changingminds.org/explanations/behaviors/ta.htm

- For more information on body language / non-verbal communication:

http://www.peaseinternational.com/
http://www.mybodylanguage.co.uk/more_on_body_language.htm
http://www.changingminds.org/techniques/body/body_language.htm

- For information on assertiveness:

http://www.assertiveness.org.uk/
http://www.bbc.co.uk/dna/h2g2/A2998551

- For information on conflict resolution:

http://www.mindtools.com/pages/article/newLDR_81.htm

- For information on influencing styles:

http://www.ezinearticles.com/?Understanding-The-Different-Influencing-Styles&id=340096

 # Time for review and reflection

This is your space to log your reflections on this chapter, to think about what you have learnt, how you will use it and what else you need to find out.

What were the key learning points of this chapter?

What are your strengths in the areas covered by this chapter?

What areas did you identify for development?

What have you learnt about yourself?

How will you use it?

What else do you need to learn or find out about in relation to this chapter?

4 How to Nurture Yourself During the Developmental Process

Overview – what's in this chapter?

- Why do you need to upgrade your self-nurturing skills?
- Living independently
- Managing your money
- Managing your time
- Handling stress and developing relaxation techniques
- Getting to sleep
- Looking after your health, including diet, exercise and health problems
- Accessing help and support
- Follow-up activities, further reading and websites to look up
- Time for review and reflection

Why do you need to upgrade your self-nurturing skills?

Try completing this short self-scoring test, to assess your own level of confidence in relation to your nurturing skills, to help you complete your course successfully.

Activity: Why do you need to read this chapter?	
You need to self score each question on a scale from 0 to 10, where 0 is low and 10 is high.	
1. How confident are you about living independently?	
2. How are you with managing your money?	
3. How good are you at getting to places on time?	

4. How likely are you to meet deadlines that are set for you?	
5. How good are you at managing stress?	
6. How easy do you find it to relax?	
7. How good are you at eating a balanced diet?	
8. How regularly do you exercise?	
9. How likely are you to ask for help if you have a health problem?	
10. How aware are you of the support systems available to you?	
Total score	

Interpretation

What did you score?

- Less than 50%   You definitely will find a lot of help in this chapter.
- 50%–75%   There is still plenty to learn in this chapter.
- 75%–100%   You are very confident – read on to confirm your understanding.

Studying in higher education can be tough! There are many pressures to achieve and succeed and many of you will be living in a new situation with new people, perhaps living independently for the first time. Skills such as washing, cooking and cleaning may seem somewhat mundane when starting a university course in your chosen discipline, but they are essential for completing it.

What we are looking at in this chapter are **survival skills**. Too many students fall by the wayside because they are not equipped to deal with the experience of higher education. Some get into debt, others get sick through poor diet and lack of exercise, while others develop destructive behaviour patterns.

You may, depending upon your course, have far less contact time with academic staff than you were used to in school or college. Therefore developing the ability to live and work independently will become very important. For others these will be skills that you already have.

In this chapter we will look at a range of issues, including the problems living independently, managing your money, managing your time, handling stress, developing relaxation techniques and getting to sleep, together with the need to look after your health, including diet, exercise and dealing with health problems. Finally there are some follow-on activities, some suggested further reading, websites to look up, and some space for review and reflection.

Living independently

Activity: What is good and bad about independent living?

There are many pros and cons related to living away from home. If you are doing this for the first time, try working through the following questions:

- What are you looking forward to?

- What are you not looking forward to or are most anxious about?

Adjusting to living independently

For many students, the biggest adjustment they have to make when moving into higher education is learning to live independently from family and friends for the first time. The good news is that you can make a lot of new friends and that these new friendships are made with others who are in a similar situation to yourself.

If you make good friends they will become your support network, so this is a priority and will probably happen quite naturally (see also Chapter 1 which looks at the transition into higher education and gives you ideas on meeting new people).

Other considerations include managing your money, accommodation, getting to sleep, and dealing with domestic chores such as shopping, cooking, washing and cleaning – all issues which are discussed in this chapter.

Living in a student room

A university or college room can look very bare when you move in, and a good start is to make it your own space. Some ideas include:

- Bring some things from home such as posters, books, mugs, music system, and maybe a potted plant.

- Invest in an electric kettle and some supplies of tea and coffee – it will save you money in the long run and may encourage visitors to your room.

- Make friends with your neighbours. They need not become your closest friends, but it is good to be on friendly terms with them, to be mutually supportive and to avoid any unnecessary conflict.

- Leave your door open when you want company and close it when you want to work. Others will soon get the message and, if not, a 'do not disturb' sign works wonders.

It is a question of defining your space and making your room a 'home from home'. It will be your lounge, bedroom and study for the next year and you are going to spend quite a bit of time there, working and entertaining, so it's a good idea to make it as comfortable as possible.

> ### Activity: What do I want to take?
>
> If you are going to be living in a student room in 'halls' or a college, try making a list of things you will want to take with you.

Living in a shared house

Living in a shared house can bring special problems in terms of sharing common spaces such as the lounge (if there is one), bathroom and kitchen. Common areas of conflict are the recurring 'washing-up crisis' and people not cleaning the bath. While these are irritating, more serious problems can occur over shared payment of bills etc. Some tips for house sharing include the following:

- Hold a house meeting to agree rules at the outset – in terms of how it is going to be, who does what and how bills are to be divided etc.

- Set a really good example yourself by being respectful of others and practising what you have agreed. If the person in the next room played loud music till five in the morning and kept you awake, doing the same to him the next night is not an amicable – or effective – solution!

- Try to be on good terms with everybody, being helpful and flexible. If you are making a cuppa, why not offer to make the others one?

- Don't leave nasty little notes around the place, saying 'Who didn't do ...' or such like. It's guaranteed to antagonise your housemates and poison the atmosphere. It is better to try and approach things directly and in an adult rational manner. See Chapter 3 on interpersonal skills.

- Assert yourself appropriately, when it is right to do so. See also Chapter 3 on developing your people skills – particularly the sections on resolving conflict and on asserting yourself.

Private landlords can be highly variable in terms of the treatment you get, and some are notorious, so it's usually better to rent properties on the approved list from your university or college. However, even this may not be a guarantee of fair treatment. If you do get into problems you should seek advice from your university or college accommodation office and/or students' union welfare office.

House sharing can be a very positive experience but horror stories abound, so it is advisable to try and manage the situation from the start and to deal with problems as and when they arise. Be prepared for some rewards and some problems.

Managing your money

An ex-student told us...

A former university student told us that he had a really good time in year one, going out every evening and getting taxis back to his halls. Unfortunately he amassed a £20,000 overdraft in the process and had now dropped out of university while he was working to pay off his debts!

Making a budget and sticking to it

How much do you imagine you will spend – or do spend – a week? Completing the following activity has proved truly shocking for some students, but it's an essential starting point in achieving a realistic grasp of your finances.

Activity: Making your own budget

Try estimating how much you either will spend or expect to spend, expressing each figure in terms of a weekly amount.

Weekly expenditure	£
• Books, stationery and any other study materials you need for your course	
• Rents for lodgings, shared house, or college room or halls. Housekeeping if living at home	

• Telephone calls, Internet connection and mobile phone, etc.	
• Other bills for services including gas, electricity, etc.	
• Food prepared for you, including meals taken in the refectory, fast foods, etc.	
• Food you prepare, plus other household shopping such as cleaning materials, washing powder, toiletries, etc.	
• Clothing, repairs and renewals	
• Entertainment and social activities, drinking, cinema, gigs, etc.	
• Travel, including to and from where you stay to where you study	
• Weekends away, visiting home or friends and holidays, if you plan to get away in the vacations	
• A reasonable contingency for any unanticipated expenditure	
Weekly income	£
• Student loans	
• Grants or bursaries	
• Allowances from parents/family etc.	
• Paid work	
• Other	
How is it looking? If your budget is looking out of balance, it is time to think about how to change it. Try reading the next two subsections on minimising expenditure and maximising your earning potential, and then make a new budget.	

Minimising your expenditure

There are some really simple tips for minimising expenditure, including:

- **Think before you spend!** If you are an impulse buyer, try to develop a habit of stopping yourself and taking time to think before you spend. Do you really need it and is it a good deal? Being a financially solvent student might mean not wearing the latest fashions!

- **Where to eat?** Eating in halls or in the refectory may be cheaper than eating out. Making your own food will probably be even cheaper and may potentially be more nutritious than ready made food or takeaways. See also the section below on looking after your health.

- **Investigate student deals**. Student deals will often be cheaper and are worth looking at. Companies like to attract people while they are students in order to develop loyalty to their brand later on, but you need to shop around.

- **Do student things**. Student gigs will normally be much cheaper than commercial ones, as will student bars. Student travel is usually designed for the 'hard of pocket'. Your students' union will also know where you can get student discounts locally.

- **Manage your time.** Managing the balance between academic work, paid work and social life can really help with controlling your expenditure. See also the section below on managing your time.

Maximising your earning potential

Many students rely on part-time and vacation work in order to help support their studies. While too much paid work can seriously undermine your academic performance, a reasonable level of work can provide you with extra money and also a number of other benefits including:

- New friends, as you come into contact with another group of people.

- Valuable work experience. This is especially true if you can find something relevant to your line of study. Even at a lowly level you are likely to learn something useful.

- Savings in expenditure, particularly on entertainment. Most obviously if you are serving behind a bar rather than drinking at it!

- Discounts – working in clothing, food, book or other types of stores often means that you get really useful discounts on purchases.

- Free food – working in catering often means you get fed at the start or end of your shift.

However, some students get better paid jobs than others. See Chapters 9 to 11 for material on getting jobs and placements.

A student told us...

A student who worked in a well-known clothing store at weekends told us that when the weekend supervisor's job came up, he applied and then got the job, using the job search skills we had taught him (see Chapters 9 to 11). This increased his earnings considerably as well as providing useful managerial experience.

Managing financial problems

It's easy to say that the best way to avoid problems is to avoid debt. However, in the current climate of student loans and tuition fees, debt may be hard to avoid. The first step is to have a clear budget for your expenditure (as outlined in an earlier activity) and the second is to try to stick to it as far as possible. Remember your 'contingencies' allocation is there for **unforeseen emergencies**.

If you have real financial problems, the best advice everyone will give you is: don't avoid them. Interest and bank charges will literally compound and increase your debt. It is a good idea to talk to everyone who can help and get the best advice, including your:

- **bank**, which may be far more sympathetic than you might imagine. Ask to see a customer advisor, who will be able to talk you through the options.

- **student services department**, which will probably have either a specialised debt counsellor or at least somebody with significant experience in this area.

- **students' union**, which will have a welfare adviser who is experienced in advising upon student debt problems.

- **local Citizens Advice Bureau**, which will have specialised debt counsellors.

Managing your time

Why manage your time?

Time is unique! It is the only resource which we all have equally and it is the most valuable resource we have. Once used, it has gone forever; unlike many resources, time cannot be stored or hoarded, it cannot be borrowed and it cannot be given away.

As a student you need to plan your academic workload, employment, social life and domestic commitments so that you allocate the required amount of time to all your modules. More time may be needed for some subjects, so be sure that you are aware of your strengths and areas you need to give more time to.

Improving your time management can give you a better perspective on forthcoming activities and priorities, more opportunities to be creative, less stress, more leisure time and greater achievement of goals and objectives.

Activity: How do I use my time?

Try completing this activity as honestly as possible, in order to review how you use your time and how you could improve your time management.

Question:	Analysis: How well do I spend my time?	Strategy: What will I do to improve this?
Do I use time efficiently? How do I waste time?		
What or who distracts me from study?		
Do I need to plan out my time: <ul><li>for the year?</li><li>for the term?</li><li>for the week?</li><li>for the day?</li><li>for each piece of work?</li></ul>		
Do I waste time getting started?		
Do I make the most of spare moments?		
Do I find time passes and I do not know what has happened?		

- Reflecting on the analysis column, what are your major concerns?
- What strategies did you come up with to overcome these issues?
- Make a plan to overcome these problems and a date to review your progress. See also Chapter 2, especially the section on personal development planning.

Understanding some terminology

Understanding the following terminology can help us to develop better time management skills and gives us a vocabulary with which to discuss it:

- **Type A and Type B personality.** Are you 'high drive' (Type A) or 'low drive' (Type B)? Both obsessive 'workaholics' and committed 'lazybones' are guilty of the abuse and misuse of time. Some students do too little work and fail to achieve their goals, while some others completely overdo it and burn out.

- **Presenteism**. This is where people stay at work for an excessive number of hours and can be the result of many factors including heavy workload, inefficiency, trying to impress the boss or colleagues and an unhappy home life. Similarly, some students feel that they have to know everything or do everything to get good marks, but they tend to become confused in the process.

- **Absenteeism**. This may also be related to work or home factors such as poor motivation or commitment to a job, or domestic or family problems. Some students frequently cut classes, but how often does this benefit them in achieving their goals? Who is winning here?

- **Task mesmorisation**. This is when we allow ourselves to be side tracked, concentrating on some task or tasks to the exclusion of others. We usually do it because we feel secure in the area of mesmorisation, and because we fear the other tasks we have to do. Some students absorb themselves in a particular module or topic to the exclusion of others, while others avoid their bogey subject altogether – perhaps hoping it will go away.

- **Time bandits**. These are people who rob you of your precious time, making unreasonable demands upon it. If they stole money from your wallet or purse, how would you react? Is your time any less valuable? Controlling time bandits is essentially about asserting ourselves and our own self worth (see Chapter 3, Asserting yourself when it is appropriate). As a student there are always possibilities for happy interruptions to your studies, but make sure that you are really doing what you want to do.

- **Time structuring** is an excessive attention to the structuring of time, so that it becomes a barrier to any flexibility. Can you tell the time at any time during the day without looking at your watch? Do you say, 'But I always do this at that time'? If so, maybe it's time for a bit more flexibility.

- **Me time**. This is the time – which we all need – to think, relax, exercise and recharge our batteries. It is yours, you deserve it, and you worked for it, so take it and don't feel guilty! There is an awful tendency in modern life to feel that you should always be doing something, be it work or play, but stopping and resting are important too. It is now almost a lost art that we have to relearn.

Self-management skills

Time management is the management of the activities we engage in during our life. Time management is a key element in self-management because if you can't manage your time, then clearly it is hard to achieve anything else. Therefore, managing your time is essential to achieving your goals (see also Chapter 2 on planning your personal development).

As with managing anything else, self-management involves certain skills, including:

- setting goals / objectives.

- prioritising.

- planning.

- implementing.

- controlling.

- evaluating.

If you are both concerned about how you are spending your time and serious about improving, consider the following:

- **Commitment** – there are no gimmicks or short cuts. Sloppy time management is just a bad habit. You must be committed to doing something about it.

- **Analysis** – you must have data on where you spend your time, what your problems are, and the causes. Time logs and other forms of analysis are essential.

- **Planning** – you may be saying 'I don't have time to plan', but effective management always requires planning, whether you are managing a family budget, a business, or your studies. An hour of planning will save you many hours doing the wrong things, fighting crises and avoiding the unimportant.

- **Follow-up and re-analysis** – a plan will not work very well, no matter how good it is, if you don't monitor results, detect problems, and modify the plan accordingly.

What kind of time manager are you?

As a student it might be useful to consider yourself as a manager of your own time. Do you manage your time or does it manage you?

Activity: Fire fighter or town planner?

Contrast these two polar opposites and consider which model you feel you most closely resemble, placing yourself on the continuum below.

FIRE FIGHTER	5 – 4 – 3 – 2 – 1 – 0 – 1 – 2 – 3 – 4 – 5		TOWN PLANNER
The fire fighter is totally reactive and spends all day dealing with crises, and crisis has become a habit – a way of life. Fire fighters find it hard to delegate or to trust subordinates, in case they fail. Thus they do fail, and crisis is assured. The fire fighters have no wider vision, or big picture.			The town planner is totally proactive; everything is planned, every moment of every day, and everything has a purpose. It sounds ideal but town planners cannot recognise the need to react to a crisis, unless it has been included in their planning. Thus the town planner is totally inflexible and lacks any sensitivity to immediate issues.

Procrastination

Do you have difficulty getting started on projects, leave things till the last minute, or put off until another day what you could have done today? If the answer to any of these questions was yes, then you have a tendency to procrastinate.

Activity: Find your procrastination quotient

Take the following test to find out just how bad your problem is. Circle the number that best applies for each question.

I invent reasons and look for excuses for not acting on a problem.

Strongly agree	4	3	2	1	Strongly disagree

It takes pressure to get me to work on difficult assignments.

Strongly agree	4	3	2	1	Strongly disagree

I take half measures that will avoid or delay unpleasant or difficult tasks.

Strongly agree	4	3	2	1	Strongly disagree

I face too many interruptions and crises that interfere with accomplishing my major goals.

Strongly agree	4	3	2	1	Strongly disagree

I sometimes neglect to carry out important tasks.

Strongly agree	4	3	2	1	Strongly disagree

(Continued)

(Continued)

I schedule assignments too late to get them done as well as I know I could.

Strongly agree   4   3   2   1   Strongly disagree

I am sometimes too tired to do the work I need to do.

Strongly agree   4   3   2   1   Strongly disagree

I start new tasks before I finish old ones.

Strongly agree   4   3   2   1   Strongly disagree

When I work in groups, I try to get other people to finish what I do not.

Strongly agree   4   3   2   1   Strongly disagree

I put off tasks that I really do not want to do but I know that I must do.

Strongly agree   4   3   2   1   Strongly disagree

Scoring: Total the numbers you have circled.

Your Score: ....

Interpretation:

- If your score is below 20, you are not a chronic procrastinator and you probably have only an occasional problem.
- If your score is 21–30, you have a minor problem with procrastination.
- If your score is above 30, you procrastinate quite often and should work on breaking the habit.

The problem is that procrastination can become a habit. Some people say they just can't get started, while others leave everything to the last minute. It may well affect what kind of degree or job you get – or even if you get one at all. So if you have a problem, it's time for action!

Activity: Overcoming procrastination

- Think about the last time you procrastinated. Describe it as completely as you can. What was the task?
- What did you do rather than doing what needed to be done?

Planning your time

So far in this section we have looked at how you use and perhaps abuse your time. Students often complain early in their courses about having too much time between lectures, seminars and workshops. Yet later on there are often desperate attempts to complete assignments on time.

Part of what we have to learn, both as students and through life, is how to use our time more effectively in order to achieve our objectives. So how will you use your time in the future?

Activity: Planning your time

In order to achieve your objectives it would be useful for you to complete the following two time plans:

1. **Weekly schedule**: try taking your academic timetable and fitting in other things you have to do around it, so you can get into a workable routine. For example you might plan times to go to the library between lectures on a Monday and to do your washing after seminars on a Tuesday and so on.
2. **Work schedule**: try taking your academic year diary and fill in assignment deadlines. Then add earlier deadlines to start researching, reading and writing up each piece of work, so that your final deadlines are just for handing in.

Fix review dates in your diary in order to monitor your progress. Be prepared to change and update your plans, so that you achieve your goals.

Handling stress and developing relaxation techniques

What is stress and what causes it?

Many people complain of stress or being 'stressed out', but what is stress? Many stress symptoms can be identified, but what underlies these is more complex. Mental stress will cause physical symptoms, as for example when we complain of butterflies in our stomach before making a speech or an oral presentation. Stress is therefore a cause, while physical symptoms are effects.

Long-term stress that comes from working in a stressful environment or living in a stressful situation is frequently less perceptible or immediately apparent. We may complain of a sickly feeling, sleeping badly, or experience physical symptoms which may or may not be stress related (as in conditions such as asthma for example). We may have a stress-related illness but not necessarily relate it to our occupational or domestic stress. However, just as there is no smoke without fire, there is no effect without a cause.

Is stress necessarily bad for you? There are different kinds of stress, for example:

- **Eustress** – this is the positive stress associated with achievement and exhilaration which gives us energy and motivation.

- **Distress** – this is associated with negative feelings of helplessness, hopelessness, etc.

It is true to say but perhaps harder to accept that stress is caused not so much by what happens to us, but by the way we as individuals react to external events. For example, pressure of work is frequently blamed for stress, but so is unemployment. While some people become stressed in these situations others do not. This is not to say that excessive pressure of work or long-term unemployment are desirable, but rather that we need to understand the way in which we react to life events and, in particular, the role of anxiety, fear and phobias.

Anxiety results from personal fears which may, to a greater or lesser extent, be rational. The **flight or fight syndrome** refers to the situation in which the body produces extra adrenaline in response to perceived danger. It may lead to a classic **panic attack**, where the individual feels overwhelmed by fear or routinely to a low level 'sickly' feeling.

Fear is at the root of all anxiety feelings – it is our normal and natural emotional protection from a dangerous world but it becomes a problem when our fears are either groundless or exaggerated, as in a phobia. **Phobias** are either irrational fears, such as fearing that the sky might fall down on you, or more commonly based upon exaggerations of rational fears, such as fearing that your plane might crash.

Overcoming our fears

We need to confront unrealistic fears and get realistic fears into perspective – for example, accepting that flying is safer than crossing the road! To do this we may need to embark upon a programme of systematic relaxation, so that we can then face our fears by use of either:

- **Flooding** as exemplified by jumping in at the deep end of a swimming pool if you are scared of water, going to the top of a tall building if you fear heights, or getting straight back on a horse if you have fallen off.

- **Systematic and progressive desensitisation** is achieved by confronting fears in easy stages: doing small things first and gradually building up confidence. For example the fear of flying might be confronted first by looking at pictures of planes and then visiting airports before finally boarding a plane.

If you have a serious phobic problem or long-term unresolved anxieties, you should seek professional help. Your first port of call might well be your university or college medical centre or student services department.

Controlling our own stress

It is really important not to let stress take over your life, as not only can it seriously affect your health but also your performance in every aspect of your life. For help in controlling the day-to-day stresses of student life, some practical ideas for stress control include:

- **Learn to breathe!** Breathing is as important to stress control as it is to life itself. It was the first thing you did when you were born and the last thing you will do on this earth. A little time spent every day retraining yourself to breathe slowly and deeply from the abdomen will provide a technique which you can draw upon in any sedentary situation. Try it in lectures, seminars, in traffic jams and any time you get delayed and eventually it will become automatic. It also helps with vocal projection and public speaking. See also Chapter 7 on giving presentations.

- **Take more exercise!** Sport and exercise help to burn off surplus adrenaline and release endorphins to create a feeling of well being by changing our body chemistry. Gentle walking, cycling and swimming all provide valuable opportunities for thought and reflection, and regulate breathing – generally they are rhythmic and centring activities for the mind and body (see also the section below on building in the right kind of exercise).

- **Offload problems!** It's not good to 'bottle things up'. It is much better to share problems regularly, making time for good quality communications with friends, housemates, family, tutors, your doctor, counsellor or whoever else you feel is most appropriate.

- **Write it down!** Writing up notes, reports, or keeping a diary or journal can all be cathartic and your course may include a requirement for reflective practice for just this reason. In a sense paper can be the best counsellor, because it is absolutely neutral. Many courses now encourage various forms of reflective practice, and this too provides a space for you to write down things you think and feel. See also Chapter 5 on why reflection is important to learning.

- **Stop blaming and start accepting!** Blaming is a common activity and builds negative connections in the brain which may lead us into depression. It's well worth asking yourself who you blame, for what, and why. Try to break the blaming habit, recognising that it is preferable to achieve a positive outcome by trying to do something positive about a negative situation, rather than going on about it. A good rule is to change what you can change and accept what you can't. See also Chapter 3 on asserting yourself when it is appropriate.

- **Make time for yourself!** Good time management helps you to use your time effectively. Prioritise work, and use diaries and charts to plan your time. This should also involve creating time for you – or **me time** – which means making a date with yourself in order to unwind, relax, and get in touch with yourself. See also the previous section on managing your time.

- **Meditation** is an excellent way of creating 'me time', and involves learning techniques for relaxation and exploring the inner space of our own psyche. You may be able to learn meditation techniques through a local Buddhist group or centre.

- **Learn a relaxation technique.** Relaxation tapes and books frequently teach relaxation response techniques, in which you will learn to relax when you 'pull' a psychological trigger – usually a key word which you have learnt to associate with relaxation. **Autogenic training** teaches a particular set of mental techniques used to help with relaxation, stress control, off loading and positive thinking (Bird and Pinch, 2002; Kermani, 1996).

- **Visualise yourself not being stressed**. Visualisation links well with meditation and relaxation techniques, and involves picturing and recording how – realistically – we think things might be. If we build a picture in our mind of how we might handle a difficult situation better, we are more prepared when we meet it because we have already built some of the psychological structures of the experience. For example, if you fear examinations, visualise yourself being relaxed and confident while taking an examination. See also Chapter 2, Visualising your success and Chapter 8 on developing successful examination techniques.

- **Get professional help if you need it.** If you have serious and unresolved issues, it's good to get help with them. See the section below, Accessing help and support, for ideas on where to go and who to ask.

Activity: Overcoming stress

- Take a few minutes to review the list above.
- Consider the question: What do I need to do differently in order to avoid stress? Jot down your ideas here and make a diary date to review your progress every week.
- Keep a 'stress diary' for one month. Spend a few minutes every day first reflecting and then recording both good and bad events that have happened through the day, putting a stress level against each on a scale of 1–10. Also note what you did to control your stress and which relaxation techniques you used each day.
- Review your stress diary. After one month – perhaps before – you should be able to identify causes of stress and successful stress control strategies.

Getting to sleep

It is not unusual for new students to have sleep problems and also for these to occur before key points in academic life, such as before assignment deadlines and examinations. For most people these are short-term disruptions, however, if you have long-term unresolved sleep problems you should seek advice from your doctor or university medical centre. They may be able to help you directly or in extreme cases they could refer you to a specialist hospital sleep clinic.

A student told us…

A student told us that this was her first time living away from home and that she had serious sleep problems. She was having difficulty both getting to sleep and then waking up. She had missed a lot of morning lectures and seminars and was feeling permanently tired.

The paradox with sleep is that we routinely do it quite naturally, but when we try to do it we often seem to fail. To sleep successfully, we normally need three things:

- You need to be tired. This might sound obvious, but it's amazing how many people go to bed early the night before an exam for example and then can't sleep. So don't go to bed until you are tired.

- You need to be relaxed. This is why worrying about not sleeping keeps you awake. Fortunately there are many things you can do to help achieve a deep state of relaxation, without the use of drugs or alcohol.

- You normally need to be comfortable, although if you are very tired you may fall asleep without being so, for example when travelling.

If you can create a situation where all three states – tired, relaxed and comfortable – occur at the same time, you will almost certainly sleep. The next activity gives you some ideas which might help.

Activity: Improving your chances of getting to sleep quickly

Consider putting the following 20 points into action:

- Don't go to bed until you are tired. Early nights might be ok if you are really tired, but going to bed too early is fighting what your body is telling you.
- Avoid too much exciting late night entertainment just before attempting to sleep such as television, videos or books.
- Avoid eating too much, too late.
- Avoid caffeine altogether in the evening.
- Do eat a little to stop your blood sugar level dropping overnight and your body waking you up.
- Create a quiet time before bedtime to reflect upon the day and put it in perspective.
- Make a note of anything you have to do the next day. Use notes, lists or a diary so you don't have to remember those things all night.
- Write down any things that are on your mind before you try to sleep, as this will help to prevent you thinking about them during the night.
- Make sure that you have enough bedclothes so you won't be cold and not so many that you will overheat, because either being too hot or too cold may wake you up.
- Do set alarm clocks if you need to be up at a certain time, otherwise you may spend all night worrying about whether you will oversleep or not.
- Put a few drops of a soothing aromatherapy oil such as camomile or lavender underneath your pillow. Avoid using an oil burner overnight as the flame will give a flickering light and it is also a fire risk.
- Make yourself comfortable, perhaps starting on your back, even if this is not your normal sleeping position.
- Try to avoid thinking about sleep altogether, because it generally happens when you're not thinking about it.
- See your mission not as sleep but rather as achieving a deep state of relaxation, telling yourself that if you are relaxed, tired and comfortable then you will sleep.
- Start breathing slowly and regularly, evenly and deeply.
- Breathe down into your body rather than up into your head. This takes your attention into your body, which you want to refresh in sleep, rather than into your brain, which you want to relax.
- Focus your thoughts on your breathing, allowing any intrusive thoughts to pass through your mind, and remember always to return to thinking about your breathing.

- With every breath, feel yourself going further down, more and more into a deep state of relaxation.
- Take at least twenty such conscious breaths every night.
- When you feel ready, move into your normal sleeping position.
- If all this fails, try staying awake all night. This usually fails and results in a good night's sleep!

  1. What do you think you might do differently in order to put these ideas into action?
  2. Try making a sleep strategy incorporating the ideas you have identified as being most useful to you.
  3. Try your new sleep strategy for a week and then review your progress.

Looking after your health, including diet, exercise and health problems

If you can stay healthy, it really helps you to improve your chances of achieving your goals, both in terms of your studies and your wider goals in life. Conversely, falling ill can seriously undermine performance. Many students are quite healthy when they start their courses but fall sick during their first year due to poor nurturing skills and/or lifestyle decisions. Some students underachieve, some have to intermit (take a year or so out), while a few drop out altogether.

In this section we look at some of the things you can do to help your body stay fit and prevent health problems adversely affecting your studies. In particular we will look at diet, exercise, smoking, drinking, drugs, and dealing with health problems including sexual health. However, many health problems are stress related, so you should also see the section above on handling stress and relaxation techniques.

Improving your diet

Eating a balanced diet is standard health education advice and you will probably already know that you should get your daily share of vitamins, proteins and carbohydrates, but many students do get run down because of poor diet, particularly during their first winter away from home.

Following government advice and eating five portions of fruit and vegetables is a good start. If your shopping does not include much that is fresh and green, you might need to spend more time in the supermarket's greengrocery section. Local food markets, greengrocers, farm shops and farmers markets are also worth looking out for and can prove cheaper than the supermarket. While fruit juices can be used to supplement your fruit and vegetable intake, eating fresh rather than processed greengrocery also helps us get the trace elements we need, which are often missing from the processed alternatives.

We definitely need proteins too, but eating meat every day is both expensive and unnecessary provided you get protein from other sources such as fish, dairy products, rice, pulses and nuts. There are plenty of very healthy vegetarians! As for carbohydrates, though they are often seen simply as a filler, the body needs these for energy and you will get some vitamins as well. Potatoes, pasta and rice are good standbys for any kitchen and can be rotated for variety.

Breakfast can be the most important meal of the day. Taking a few minutes to make porridge can make for a good warming start, especially in the winter. Oats are also good for absorbing fats. Breakfast is also a good time to start adding extra fibre to the diet through cereals, but eating plenty of fruit, vegetables and whole grains through the day will also support this. Try to avoid snacking and fast foods. These tend to be relatively expensive, full of additives and often of limited nutritional value.

Plan your shopping. It is much better to have a list rather than just grabbing things that take your eye in the supermarket. Taking five minutes to make a list before you go can save a lot of time, waste and unnecessary expense. However, it is also good to look for bargains and be prepared to change your plans if something is really worth buying instead of what you had planned. In particular, fruit and vegetables get marked down if there is a glut or a sudden change in the weather. Avoiding waste is important, because it is just costing you money for nothing. So do watch those 'consume by' dates and if you buy too much of something, try to think what else you can make out of it.

Many students learn to cook at university partly through necessity, because it saves money, but also because it can be fun. You can make cooking an adventure, trying a new recipe every week. In shared accommodation it can be good idea to have a rota. Not only can this be more time efficient, as you may well only have to cook a couple of times a week, but also it can mean you have a more sociable house as people are committed to eating together. Cooking with or for friends and having the occasional dinner party can be fun – and a lot cheaper than eating out.

Activity: Are you what you eat?

1. Take a minute to think about your diet. Here are a few questions to consider:

   - Do you eat too much or too little food, or just enough to sustain you?
   - Do you get a good balance of vitamins, proteins and carbohydrates?

- Do you snack rather than eating more balanced meals?
- Do you shop well for food, getting good nutritional value for your money?

2. Try making a food plan or shopping list for the next week. How does it differ from what you ate last week?

Building in the right kind of exercise

If you want to be in really good shape for your studies, the best advice is to take regular cardiovascular exercise. This means using big muscles – as in walking, running, cycling and swimming – to work the heart and to get the blood and lymphatic systems, which help to maintain your body, working really well. While weights may help you build the body beautiful, they do not provide the heart with the right type of workout it needs to see you through life.

Physiologically, cardiovascular exercise burns off adrenaline, associated with stress responses (see section above on handling stress), and helps to release endorphins which bring feelings of pleasure. Originally known as enkephalin, endorphins have been described as the 'brain's own morphine' and as causing, among other things, the 'euphoria associated with exercise' (Pert, 1999: 349).

The standard advice is to build up slowly if you are unused to vigorous exercise. If you are an older student or have health problems it is wise to consult your doctor, who will be able to advise you.

Team sports are an obvious choice for some but if you are not the team sport type you might also consider racket sports such as tennis, squash or badminton, where getting your cardiovascular exercise can also be fun.

Walking is perhaps the simplest form of cardiovascular exercise and, if you do it regularly enough, it can be all you need to keep your heart in shape. Walking round town can be good exercise, but getting out to the hills and vales at the weekend can also be a rewarding hobby. Walking with others can be a good and sociable activity, but walking alone also provides a good time to think and reflect. Even if you have a car, you don't have to drive everywhere. Do consider the park and walk option which will both give you exercise and save you money.

Running is an excellent form of cardiovascular exercise but can be very hard on the joints, especially if you are road running. Investing in the right footwear can really help to overcome the tendency to develop joint problems. If you have problems in this area, swimming is a clear alternative as it also provides excellent cardiovascular exercise but takes the weight off your joints. Swimming is usually a cheaper option than many other sports, needs little equipment and local pools will often have a discounted student rate.

Joining university sports groups can be a very good way of committing yourself to regular exercise and of making new and perhaps healthier friends. Alternatively, finding a training partner or buddy can also help, as there is a feeling of letting someone else down if you don't turn up. However, please remember when you don't take sufficient exercise to maintain your body you are always letting someone down – and that is you!

Activity: How fit are you?

1. Take a minute to reflect upon your own level of fitness. Here are a few questions to help you:

   - Are you currently getting more fit, staying about the same, or becoming less fit?
   - Do you get more or less puffed than friends when walking up a hill?
   - On a scale of 1 to 10, how would you rate yourself if 1 was a couch potato and 10 was an Olympic athlete?
   - Where would you like to be on that scale and where could you realistically expect to get to in, say, the next six months?

2. Make an action plan to improve your level of fitness, deciding:

   - what you want to achieve.
   - how you will go about it.
   - how you will measure your improvement.
   - when and how you will review it.

(See also Chapter 2, Planning your continuing personal development.)

Drugs, alcohol and smoking

The first thing we are going to say on this is:

we are not going to say don't!

The reason for this is that we believe that it would clearly be counterproductive. We recognise the phenomenon of **Oedipal rebellion**, which is the tendency for the child to rebel against the parent, so we are definitely not going to get parental with you. However, as we know that many students do have problems in these areas we are going to discuss them and then allow you decide what you want to do.

Even the most rudimentary study of anatomy and physiology reveals the human body to be an amazing machine, capable of achieving great physical and mental feats. It has immense power to maintain and even repair itself, given the right encouragement in terms of environment, diet, exercise, etc. You may perhaps see 'your body as a temple' yet some students choose to adopt destructive behaviour patterns as represented by smoking, excessive drinking and drug abuse. Why should this be so?

We want to suggest to you that people adopt destructive behaviour patterns because they are unhappy with themselves as they are. Drugs (including nicotine and alcohol) offer the promise of escape from ourselves, making us something else – more than we otherwise would be – and also perhaps suggest social acceptability and being 'one of the gang'. So what is cool about being 'off your face' or reeking of nicotine?

Excessive alcohol intake is sometimes seen as the undergraduates' birthright, and one of the authors of this book was a willing and guilty victim of that particular mythology. However, let's examine the evidence. Alcohol is frequently associated with having a good time in pubs, clubs, at parties and so on. However, it is neither the same as pleasure nor does it assure pleasure, because physiologically it actually depresses the central nervous system.

In many ways alcohol is the drug of denial because it helps us to avoid thinking about our problems, hence expressions such as 'drown your sorrows' or being 'off your face' or 'out of your head'. While moderate drinking may form part of a normal social life, persistent habitualised heavy drinking may lead to alcoholism, which in turn will cause major damage to the liver and other vital organs together with cognitive degeneration. Walking through most city centres, it is all too easy to see the results of alcoholism laid bare before our eyes.

Smoking is probably the worst thing you can do to your lungs, heart and circulatory system but, again, one of the authors of this book used to do that too. It is clearly a very expensive hobby and increasingly socially unacceptable. However, once you start that nicotine addiction is an itch you just have to scratch. This was recognised by Carr (1995). He also recognised the association between the act of smoking and acts of pleasure, such as smoking after food or after sex. Carr offers an effective non-medical route to giving up, but there are also the well-tried patches and gums which can be obtained commercially from chemists and sometimes on free prescription from health advisers and primary care providers.

Non-prescription narcotic drugs are, by definition, mind affecting. They variously offer a 'heightened sense of reality', the ability to dance all night or to simply 'chill out'. Many students experiment with non-prescription drugs. There is a perceived glamour but we need to recognise the existence of a well-developed commercial market, in which some students are not only users but also dealers. They may appear as friends offering a service, but rather it is an exploitative commercial transaction offered by those who at that point in time need a fix more than you do. Most students who experiment do not get addicted but some do and, like Russian roulette, that is the risk you take.

Activity: Are my behaviour patterns destructive?

1. Take a minute to consider your own behaviour. In particular:

   - Do you drink excessively? If you answered yes, why do you think this is? What is the payoff for you from doing this?
   - Do you smoke? If you said yes, can you say why you started? Would you like to stop?
   - Do you use non-prescription narcotic drugs, occasionally or regularly? Can you say why? What is the payoff for you in doing this?
   - Do you have any other destructive behaviour patterns such as eating disorders?

2. If you have identified any areas where you feel you need help, please read the following section and the end of chapter material, where you will find sources of help.

A student told us...

A student who was six months into his course told us that he was having problems with coursework because he was drug and alcohol dependant and in financial difficulties. He said he was so confused he couldn't think anymore or do his work. We referred him to our student services department which arranged long-term counselling and other support. He stuck at it and, although it took him longer than the rest of his cohort, he eventually graduated successfully.

Dealing with health problems

The incidence of health problems can clearly be minimised by nurturing yourself as we have suggested in this chapter. Your accommodation, managing your money and your stress, together with a good diet and exercise all help – but we are only human.

Many complaints are stress related, and it is no coincidence that the word disease is formed of 'dis' and 'ease'. If we are **dis-eased** we are likely to become diseased, so dealing with stress, anxiety, fear, phobias and depression is important. In general, dealing with health worries promptly will help to avoid further stress. If you have health worries, an early trip to the university or college medical centre is clearly advisable.

Sexual health is a particular area of concern for many students. The use of condoms can significantly help to reduce both the likelihood of catching sexually transmitted diseases (STDs) – including the HIV virus – and the incidence of unwanted or unplanned pregnancies, which could seriously affect your studies. You may find that sexual health advice and condoms are available for free from your university or college medical centre and/or from a university/college or public health project.

Problems and fears in the area of sexual health should not be ignored, but embarrassment is a big factor here. However, the staff who work in university medical centres and the STD clinics of local hospitals will be especially used to dealing with patients in this area. If you have any doubts or concerns you should talk these over with them as soon as possible. Failing to treat STDs can not only mean you pass them on to others but can also lead to long-term health problems.

Accessing help and support

The first port of call for many problems will be your personal tutor or course leader. They will most likely be quite experienced in many of the problems which regularly occur in student lives. They will often be able to refer you to the most appropriate source of help. It is also important for them to know about what is happening to you as personal problems tend to impinge upon studies and they may have to argue your case in examination boards if your performance suffers.

For accommodation and financial problems contact your:

- Student Services Department.

- Student Union's welfare adviser or debt counsellor.

- local Citizens' Advice Bureau.

For health problems contact:

- your Student Medical Centre or the general practitioner with whom you are registered.

- the local STD clinic for help with sexual health.

Overall, there is a lot of help on offer, but you have to be prepared to access it. Pride can sometimes be a barrier but there is no shame in asking for help. We all need support at times and it is sometimes the mark of the successful student that he or she can seek help and guidance when it is needed.

Follow-up activities

TIME FOR ACTION – CHECKLIST

Have you:

- considered what you need to do to upgrade your self-nurturing skills?
- thought through the transition to living independently?
- made plans for managing your time effectively so as to achieve your goals?
- calculated a budget to help you with managing your money?
- learnt methods for handling stress and developed relaxation techniques?
- developed techniques for getting to sleep and sleeping soundly?
- given sufficient attention to your health, including diet, exercise and health problems?
- made yourself aware of sources of help and support?

Further reading

Bird, J. and Pinch, C. (2002) *Autogenic Therapy*. Dublin: Newleaf.

Cameron, S. (2008) *The Business Student's Handbook*, 4th edition. Harlow: Pearson.

Carr, A. (1995) *The Only Way to Stop Smoking Permanently*. London: Penguin Health Care & Fitness.

Chopra, D. (2001) *Perfect Health*. London: Bantam.

Cottrell, S. (2008) *The Study Skills Handbook*, 3rd edition. Basingstoke: Palgrave (pp. 74–83).

Feldman, R. (2000) *Power Learning: Strategies for Success in College and Life*. Maidenhead: McGraw-Hill Higher Education.

Kermani, K. (1996) *Autogenic Training*. London: Souvenir Press.

Lee-Davies, L. (2007) *Developing Work and Study Skills*. London: Thomson.

Pert, C. (1999) *Molecules of Emotion*. London: Pocket Books.

Pert, C. (2007) *Everything You Need To Know To Feel Good*. London: Hay House UK Ltd.

Smith, H. W. (1998) *The 10 Natural Laws of Time and Life Management*. London: Nicholas Brearley Publishing.

Websites to look up

- For help with money/student finances, health, drugs, etc.:

http://www.nusonline.co.uk/info/

- For help with financial support from the Department for Innovation, Universities and Skills:

http://www.dius.gov.uk

- For information on student loans from Student Finance Direct:

http://www.studentfinancedirect.co.uk/portal/page?_pageid=53,1259548&_dad=portal&_schema=PORTAL

- For information on health, including mental health issues:

http://www.nhsdirect.nhs.uk/
http://www.bbc.co.uk/health/
http://www.studenthealth.co.uk/

Time for review and reflection

This is your space to log your reflections on this chapter, to think about what you have learnt, how you will use it and what else you need to find out.

What were the key learning points of this chapter?

What are your strengths in the areas covered by this chapter?

What areas did you identify for development?

What have you learnt about yourself?

How will you use it?

What else do you need to learn or find out about in relation to this chapter?

PART 2 HOW TO DEVELOP YOUR ACADEMIC SKILLS

How do you Learn and How do you Know What is Required of you?

Overview – what's in this chapter?

- Why do you need to upgrade your learning skills?
- Understanding how you learn and your own learning styles
- Why is reflection important to learning?
- Developing critical thinking skills
- Mind mapping, brainstorming and creativity
- Understanding assessment
- Completing group assignments successfully
- Follow-up activities, further reading and websites to look up
- Time for review and reflection

Why do you need to upgrade your learning skills?

Try completing this short self-scoring test, to assess your own level of confidence in relation to developing your learning skills to help you complete your course successfully.

Activity: Why do you need to read this chapter?

You need to self score each question on a scale from 0 to 10, where 0 is low and 10 is high.

1. How good do you consider you are at learning?	
2. How often do you take time to reflect upon what you have learnt?	
3. How often do you take time to reflect upon how you learn?	

(Continued)

(Continued)

4. How good are you at developing critical arguments and not just taking things you read or hear at face value?	
5. How good are you at taking notes?	
6. How good are you at analysing a problem you are given?	
7. How good are you at thinking creatively?	
8. How likely are you to do exactly what an assignment asks you to do?	
9. How good are you at completing assignments on time?	
10. How confident do you feel about leading or participating in a team in order to complete a group assignment successfully?	
Total score	

Interpretation

What did you score?

- Less than 50%   You definitely will find a lot of help in this chapter.
- 50%–75%   There is still plenty to learn in this chapter.
- 75%–100%   You are very confident – read on to confirm your understanding.

We all learn, not only in education of course but throughout our lives. However, sometimes we could do it more efficiently and more effectively. In higher education it is going to be important that you learn effectively if you are going to achieve your goals. Your time is valuable, so learning efficiently makes sense.

In this chapter we will look at how we learn, how we can improve our learning skills and in particular: why reflection is important to learning, developing critical thinking skills, note taking, mind mapping, brainstorming and creativity. We will also explore the problems of understanding assessment and of working in, or leading, teams in order to complete group assignments successfully. Finally there are some follow-on activities, some suggested further reading, websites to look up, and some space for review and reflection.

Understanding how you learn and your own learning styles

To understand how we learn, it is useful to see learning as a process. As with any other process it can be broken down into stages. Understanding each stage

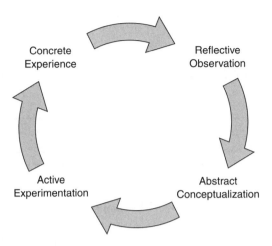

Figure 5.1 Kolb learning cycle
Source: Kolb and Fry, 1975

and our relevant strengths and weaknesses can really help us to develop our own learning.

Kolb and Fry (1975; Kolb, 1984) have suggested that there is a learning cycle (see Figure 5.1). Learning can occur at any point in the cycle and there is, therefore, no 'right way' of learning. Newton was supposedly hit by a falling apple and through reflection developed the theory of gravity, which can be tested by **active experimentation**. However, he might have started the process by reflecting upon what would happen if an apple fell, formulating a theory as to why it would happen and then testing it in an experiment which would then lead to a **concrete experience**.

We don't all learn in the same way. Honey and Mumford (1982) have developed four **learning styles** which can be plotted against the stages of the learning cycle as shown in the following table.

Kolb learning cycle	Honey and Mumford learning styles
1. Concrete Experience	Activists
2. Reflective Observation	Reflectors
3. Abstract Conceptualization	Theorists
4. Active Experimentation	Pragmatists

Honey and Mumford (1982) also suggest that we may favour particular learning styles and that our learning styles may develop over time as a result of our experience of learning.

Activity: How do you learn?

1. Consider the learning styles introduced by Honey and Mumford (1982) in terms of how you learn:

Activists involve themselves fully without bias in new experiences and revel in new challenges.	**Reflectors** stand back and observe new experiences from different angles. They collect data, reflect on it, and then come to a conclusion.
Theorists adapt and apply their observations in the form of logical theories. Tend to be perfectionists.	**Pragmatists** are keen to try out new ideas, approaches and concepts to see if they work.

2. Try to allocate one of the following statements to each of the descriptors above. You can give more than one of the descriptors to the same statement if that seems right for you.

   - Most like me
   - Fairly like me
   - A bit like me
   - Nothing like me

3. Consider what impact this knowledge will have for your studies. There are two potential outcomes:

   - You may decide that knowing how you learn, you will try to 'play to your strengths', using those methods which come most naturally to you.
   - Alternatively, you may decide to try and develop those methods of learning which you are least likely to use at the moment.

Understanding and developing your learning styles is an important step towards becoming an effective student. However, it is quite likely that your learning styles will change and develop during your life – especially so while you are in higher education.

A student told us...

A student told us after completing the Honey and Mumford learning styles questionnaire that he had done the same test two years earlier at college but that his learning styles had changed. Through discussion we established that it was his experience of education that had encouraged this development.

What is your attitude to study? In Chapter 1 we asked you to think about your motivation to learn (Recognising your own motivation to learn, grow and develop). If you can't remember what you said, it might be helpful to refer back to what you wrote there. We believe that your motivation will tend to condition everything else you do in education as well as in life in general.

We also see that students fall into two broad categories:

- **Optimistic learners** – who tend to see learning as an opportunity to learn, grow and develop. They often see learning as fun, an adventure or a positive experience.

- **Pessimistic learners** – who tend to see learning as a requirement which must be fulfilled. They often see it as a chore, a bore and a generally negative experience and frequently are looking to do the minimum required.

Activity: Are you an optimistic or pessimistic learner?

1. Consider your previous experience of education. Were you more of an optimistic learner or a pessimistic learner?
2. What is your attitude to your current studies?
3. Does your attitude need to change? If so, how?

Why is reflection important to learning?

Reflection can be seen as an essential part of the learning process (as outlined in the previous section of this chapter). The reasons for reflection include:

- Making sense of what we have studied – in other words, what does it mean?

- Considering what we think about what we have learned – in other words, is it any use and what do we feel about it emotionally?

- Seeing how what we have learned fits together with other knowledge and ideas.

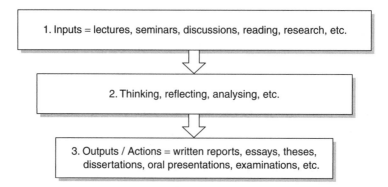

Figure 5.2   Three-stage model of reflection

Reflection is a recurring theme in this book, but what is the point of reflection? According to Moon (1999) reflection is linked with the process of learning:

> Reflection is a form of mental processing that we use to fulfil a purpose or achieve some anticipated outcome. It is applied to gain better understanding of relatively complicated or unstructured ideas and is largely based on the reprocessing of knowledge, understanding and possibly emotions that we already process.

Within the context of higher education, reflection can be viewed as fitting into a three-stage model (see Figure 5.2).

As a student you may often feel bombarded with inputs and unable to make sense of them in your outputs, be it in reports, presentations or in the examination hall. It is easy to spend too much time at stage one, and not to take the time to think about and reflect upon what you have learnt. The journey that you are asked to make in higher education is that from **surface learning** to **deep learning**. Completing the next activity will clarify what we mean by these terms.

Activity: Are you a deep or surface learner?

1.   Have a look at the levels of learning below suggested by Moon (1999).
2.   Where do you feel that you are in the hierarchy?

Transformational learning ⇧		Meaningful, reflective, restructured by the learner, creative

Work with the meaning ⇧	Deep learning	Meaningful, reflective, well structured
Making meaning ⇧		Meaningful, well integrated, ideas linked
Making sense ⇧	Surface learning	Reproduction of ideas, ideas not well linked
Noticing ⇧		Memorising representation

3. Now have a look at the following distinctions (adapted from Entwistle and Marton, 1984).

Surface approach to learning

- Intention simply to reproduce parts of the content.
- Accepting ideas and information passively.
- Concentrating only on assessment requirements.
- Not reflecting on purpose or strategy.
- Memorising facts and procedures routinely.
- Failing to distinguish guiding principles or patterns.

Deep approach to learning

- Intention to understand material for oneself.
- Interacting vigorously and critically with the content.
- Relating ideas to previous knowledge and experience.
- Using organising principles to integrate ideas.
- Relating evidence to conclusions.
- Examining the logic of the argument.

4. What could you do to deepen your learning?

Understanding how you learn, and deepening your learning, will be a major determinant of how you develop in higher education and beyond. Reflection is not only a key part of the learning process but also a key element in the developmental process.

Learning and development are clearly interrelated. How could we develop without learning in the process, and how could we learn without developing in that process?

Because we tend to learn in small bite-sized chunks, there is the question of how it all fits together. Imagine standing really close to a brick wall so that you could only see a few bricks right in front of your face. What you are looking at may be hard to determine, but by standing back you may see that it's a house or a hotel or another type of construction.

The concept of **Gestalt** comes from the German word that corresponds, approximately, to structure or pattern. The concept was first developed in Germany during the early twentieth century by the so-called **Berlin School** of writers. Later Perls (1951), who was born in Berlin but later moved to the United States, developed Gestalt as a form of therapy focusing on the 'here and now'.

In Gestalt, the structure or pattern is explained by the **SOR model**:

S	=	**Stimulus pattern**	**What affects me.**
O	=	**Perceptual organisation**	**How I deal with it.**
R	=	**Response based upon perception**	**What I do about it.**

Gestalt recognises insight, which is its central concept. More commonly we see the example of Archimedes discovering his famous principle on the displacement of water when sitting in the bath. 'Eureka' he supposedly cried in a flash of insight. This is, potentially, where Gestalt leads us to – by seeing how the evidence links and connects we come to a Eureka moment. **Mind mapping** (see section below, Mind mapping, brainstorming and creativity) can be a useful tool both for reflecting upon our studies and revealing the picture as suggested in Gestalt.

Activity: Reflecting upon your studies?

1. Try drawing a mind map or diagram which expresses the following steps:

   - Take an idea, theory or concept from your studies and try to link it first to the topic it forms a part of.
   - Next draw a link to the topic of the module it comes from.
   - Now link the module to the rest of your course.
   - Finally link your course to your own life as expressed in your personal development plan (see Chapter 2).

2. Sit back and have a look at your diagram. What sense does the original idea, theory or concept make in the context of your studies?

Developing critical thinking skills

Handling the intellectual argument

In higher education it is particularly important to question everything you read, are told or discover and not to take it at face value – rather, deal with knowledge critically. The golden rule is that **all knowledge is provisional** and can be overtaken by both new discoveries and advances in thinking.

There is an old joke which suggests that an expert is someone who understands all the latest misconceptions. The trap is to fall into believing that the latest knowledge is probably correct, when history clearly shows that most accepted knowledge is overturned eventually. Therefore, good academic work is objective, critical and grounded in theory that can be justified.

A student told us...

A student complained after a lecture which had been both full of theories and systematic in its criticism of each of them, 'Why do you teach us all these old theories if they are all wrong?'.

This is a good question which deserved a good answer. The answer was that each theory showed the development of thinking in that field and that understanding the development of theory and critique was to understand where we are now – and why.

The science of knowledge

In order to handle intellectual arguments successfully in your academic work, it is important for you to have an appreciation of a number of critical concepts. **Epistemology** is the science of knowledge which looks at how knowledge is constructed and asks us to consider two critical questions:

- How do I know what I know?

- How do I know that what I know is true?

These questions are perhaps at first sight simple and you may feel them unworthy of consideration, but consider for example quoting a simple statistic in your work. How do you know it is true? Perhaps you found it in a book, but does that make it true? If it was taken from British Government data, does that make it true? How was the data collected, analysed and presented? How could you validate the work? The questions are potentially endless and may sometimes seem quite pointless, but understanding why they need to be asked is the key.

Handling the intellectual arguments successfully, therefore, starts with the proposition that knowledge is not necessarily truth. This is because a proposition only holds until it is disproved. For example the earth is flat and the sun goes round it – or does it? There was a time when that was the perceived wisdom, but now we know better. The implication is, as stated earlier, that **all knowledge is provisional**.

We need to clearly distinguish between two types of statement which you will definitely be making in your academic work:

- **Positive statements** are those supported by evidence or examples. A positive statement supported by evidence is one which can be defended on that basis.

- **Normative statements** are statements of what is merely thought to be true. A normative statement can be protected by the use of a **caveat**, one of those small words such as 'perhaps', 'might' or 'maybe'.

Activity: Writing positive and normative statements

1. Try to write a positive statement.

2. How can your positive statement be supported, i.e. with evidence?

3. Try to write a normative statement.

4. Have you covered yourself by the use of suitable caveats?

This leads us to the question, is a positive statement ultimately possible? When we talk of knowledge about markets, we must bear in mind that we find it hard both to define a market and to predict its behaviour. Thus, is our knowledge merely belief?

This in turn leads us to another important distinction:

- **Objectivity** – to be objective requires us to exclude all of our own opinions.

- **Subjectivity** – allows for opinion. For example, take the statement: 'it was a good film'. In this case 'good' is a **value judgement**.

A **value judgement** embodies our opinions and there is limited scope for them in academic work. If you were writing a lab report on a chemical reaction there would clearly be little value in saying how you felt about it. However, if you were asked to write a critique of a film, it might be valid to include your subjective opinions towards the end of an otherwise objective analysis. However, when including our own value judgements we must always make it absolutely clear that is what they are.

The question then is, can knowledge ever be completely **value free** and, therefore, totally objective? The point of this question is exemplified by the problem of collecting social data through questionnaires when the questions embody the values of the designer. See also Chapter 6, Conducting primary source research.

Knowledge can be seen to advance as a result of two alternative processes:

- **Deductive logic** or **deduction** involves taking a theory and testing it empirically to verify or refute it. We may start by deciding what we expect to discover, but the danger is that we may exclude evidence which does not fit our hypothesis. Popper (1989) introduced the idea of **conjecture and refutation**. He argues that a **thesis** is postulated and becomes more certain with each positive replication. When it is successfully refuted, it must be either abandoned or refined. For example Newton's law of gravity was reinforced by each incidence of something falling to earth, but had to be refined with the discovery of gases that are lighter than air. A helium balloon clearly does not fall to earth like an apple falling from a tree.

- **Inductive logic** or **induction** involves accumulating evidence in support of a proposition, i.e. arguing from specific instances to produce a generalised formula. However, the proposition is never proved because of the possibility of finding other, opposing, evidence. For example smoking is generally accepted as a major cause of lung cancer, because of the strong statistical correlation between smoking and the incidence of lung cancer. However, not all smokers develop the disease and not all sufferers smoke. While the proposition may be broadly accepted as correct, it is clear that there are other factors at work. Arguing from a single instance to make a generalised formula is never acceptable in academic work because, as Popper (1989) has suggested, it is by repetition that we gain certainty and by refutation that we lose it.

How knowledge is acquired or developed can be seen to derive from three processes:

- **Empiricism** – empiricists hold that the only valid source of knowledge is that which can be experienced. Knowledge is, therefore, knowable and the world discoverable. However, for empiricists no hypothesis is effectively possible and thus nothing can be known unless it can be experienced.

- **Rationalism** – rationalists reject empiricism in favour of either inductive or deductive logic. Rationalism involves reasoning and, therefore, assumption which may be wrong. However, the danger is that rationalism may lead to value-laden theory.

- **Dialectics** – date back as far as the ancient Greek philosophers, whose preferred form of the dialectic was literally an argument or conversation. All dialectics involve a process of **thesis** and **antithesis**, or argument and counter argument. In the nineteenth century a dialectical approach was adopted by Marx and Engels (1967). In Marx's materialist conception of the history of western civilisation, he argues that society developed by stages as a result of its contradictions. Class against class, conflict leading to development and further contradiction.

An important advance in the development of epistemology has been the idea of **paradigms** which was developed by Kuhn (1970). A paradigm is a set of ideas which is internally consistent and can make real sense when you study it. However, a problem arises where there are competing paradigms or idea sets, such as in religion or politics, where we are offered alternative versions of the truth by advocates of different paradigms. Some examples of competing paradigms within fields of study or belief are:

- **Politics**: conservatism, liberalism, socialism, communism, anarchism, environmentalism, etc.

- **Psychology**: behaviourism and cognitive psychology.

- **Economics**: Keynesianism, Monetarism and Marxism.

- **Religion/belief systems**: Buddhism, Christianity, Hinduism, Islam, Sikhism, Humanism, etc.

Kuhn (1970) argues that revolutions in science occur when a number of anomalies challenge an idea set. The great 'scientific revolution' occurred in the seventeenth century. Copernicus had theorised that the sun did not revolve around the earth but that the reverse was true in the 1540s. After almost two centuries and the work of Kepler, Galileo and Newton, the theory became generally accepted. This acceptance was slow in coming as the theory challenged not only conventional scientific wisdom, such as it was, but also the ideas of the church.

Evaluating what you read

The clear message of this section is to be critical, recognise how the knowledge was acquired and perhaps to challenge it. Some terms which will be useful to you in recognising what you are reading include:

- **Thesis** – this is an intellectual argument, although the term is used more often for a long piece of work which would contain your argument or arguments.

- **Antithesis** – this is the counter argument to a thesis.

- **Synthesis** – this is a combining of arguments.

In higher education we don't expect you to just take what you read at face value but to treat it critically, remembering the earlier point that all knowledge is provisional. Some of the critical questions that you might want to ask are:

1. What is the main area under review or discussion?

2. What are the main findings?

3. Where does the author's data and evidence come from, and are they appropriate and sufficient for the purpose of their argument?

4. What are the main issues raised by the author?

5. What questions are raised and how well are these questions addressed?

6. What are the major points/interpretations made by the author in terms of the issues raised?

7. Is the text balanced? Is it fair or biased and, if the latter, how is it biased?

8. How does all this relate and compare to:

    - other literature on this topic?

    - your own experience, ideas and views?

9. How can you summarise all of the above points?

10. What are your conclusions about the literature?

(Adapted from: CAPLITS Centre for Professional Literacies)

> ### Activity: Reviewing literature from your course
>
> - Start this activity by identifying an item of reading for your course.
> - Read and review this critically, using the ten questions in the critical questions list above as a basis for your analysis.
> - How does the work look to you after this critical review?
> - Try to make this critical approach the way that you normally approach academic literature, developing a 'critical eye' in the process.

Mind mapping, brainstorming and creativity

Our amazing brains

In developing a sound study technique it is useful to consider how your brain works. We normally have 10,000,000,000 brain cells at our disposal. These cells are connected by *boutons* (or buttons) which are the product of our life experiences which have been processed and encoded by our brains. Every life experience has been stored away and, while we never forget them, our practical problem as students is recalling information as and when we want it.

Work on monkeys by Nobel Prize-winning neuroscientists Hubel and Weisel (1977) recognised the extent to which we build our own brains through a process of **pruning**. For example a child learning the piano will develop those parts of the brain controlling motor drive to the fingers, whereas a child concentrating on football will develop other parts controlling foot and head movement. More recently work by neuroscientists has shown that our bodies also have a molecular informational system which challenges the idea of an electrical synapse model (Pert, 1999: 138).

We all have an amazing piece of equipment at our disposal – a sort of super computer – which can analyse and store a range of information and direct complex motor skills such as playing sports or musical instruments, while at one and the same time monitoring and controlling our body functions though the **autonomic nervous system**. We don't have to remember to breathe, digest food or even to repair a cut finger. Our brains just take care of that, leaving us free to think and grow.

However, when we are in education we can often feel overwhelmed and overloaded with cognitive inputs, including those from lectures, seminars, reading and discussions. This is why it is important for us to develop techniques to help us if we are to achieve our goals in education and beyond.

Key words and mind mapping

The idea of mind mapping was introduced by Buzan (1974) and avoids the standard **linear** technique of note taking in favour of concentrating on the quality of our encoding of information. This involves drawing **mind maps**, in which we put the topic at the centre of our notes rather than at the top, and then work outwards from the central topic in expanding branches.

As we identify **key words** we make a connection not only on the paper, but also in our brain. As we make these connections we are inserting psychological triggers, which can be pulled when we want to recall not only the key words, but also other information that is filed away with them. We can see the brain as being similar to a computer or filing cabinet – if files are clearly named and filed away in a logical sequence, the process of retrieving information becomes much easier.

Mind mapping can also be used to enhance our powers of creativity. Try putting a problem at the centre of a piece of paper and then working out from it in different directions. This helps us to expand our **lateral thinking** and again gets away from the **linear thinking** which is associated with lists and formal reports.

When writing up a formal report or essay, try to **brainstorm** all the main points first. Then order your points into a logical sequence and write around them. Your key words may become your sub-headings. Similarly, you can use a mind map to structure the content for an oral presentation (see also Chapter 7, Writing up reports and essays, Structuring material and constructing your arguments, and Giving effective presentations).

When revising for examinations, try reducing all your topics to mind maps. If you use these for revision you can improve your recall in the examination. Brainstorm your key words in the examination, not only will they give your essays structure but you will also avoid the tendency to dry up (see also Chapter 8 on examination revision).

Activity: Making mind maps work for you

- Identify a topic from your course and reduce your notes to a mind map. Use colour, highlighting, drawings or diagrams to make it really memorable.
- File your mind map away for a couple of days and then try to re-draw it from memory. You may be surprised at how much you remember.
- Consider how you can use this technique in your studies.

Understanding assessment

Why do we have assessment?

If you are struggling to complete a piece of work by the deadline or revising for a dreaded examination, you may well be asking, 'why do we have to have assessments?'. Here are a few suggestions:

- To monitor your progress and development.

- To measure your own performance.

- To show what you have learnt.

- To get feedback on your ability.

- To allow for progression through your course.

- To acknowledge your achievement (as at graduation ceremony).

- To give access to higher qualifications.

- To get a good job or move into the area of employment you want.

- To allow you to progress in life.

It is important to see that, although the process may feel somewhat painful at times, there are positive reasons for going through it, plus positive outcomes to focus upon. This clearly links back to what you said about your motivation in the activity in Chapter 1 and helps in planning your continuing personal development, which was covered in Chapter 2.

Assessment can either be formative or summative, as outlined below:

- **Formative assessment** can take place at any time during your course and its purpose is to provide you with feedback about how well you are progressing in your studies and also to provide you with guidance as to topics that you may need to focus on before the summative assessment takes place.

- **Summative assessment** occurs at the end of a module or a course and this assessment will result in the final mark awarded for your work. It is important to seek formative assessment/feedback if you need help to ensure that your work is of the appropriate standard before summative assessment takes place.

What do degree classifications mean?

If you are new to higher education you may be unsure as to what your marks mean. The following table can be used as a guide to what your tutors are trying to tell you:

Mark	Degree class	Your work is
70+	First class	Excellent
60–69	Second class (division 1) more commonly known as 2.1	Good
50–59	Second class (division 2) more commonly known as 2.2	OK
40–49	Third class (3rd)	Passable
0–39	Fail or refer	Poor

In Britain it is uncommon for staff to mark into the upper end of the percentage range. This can often confuse new students, and especially international students, if they are used to markers using all of the available range.

Activity: What sort of grades do you want?

- Take a few minutes to consider what sort of grades or degree class you realistically think you could achieve.
- What do you need to do to get the grades you want?
- Is this part of your personal development plan?

Building grade achievements into your personal development plan can bring real dividends (see Chapter 2, Planning your continuing personal development), particularly if you set realistic grade outcomes, detail what you need to do to achieve them, and set regular times for review. Setting a single review date after grades are issued will be too late, because it is what you do day-by-day and week-by-week which ultimately will determine your success.

Understanding your assessments

It may sound too obvious to say, but being absolutely clear about what you have to do is essential to completing your assessments successfully. Don't be surprised if you find your assessments hard; in higher education the work is meant to be difficult in order to stretch you, but not impossibly so.

There should always be a written assignment brief and this should be clear. If you don't understand what you have to do just ask your tutors. Beware of relying on your peers' interpretation of the assignment brief. Many a myth has been fostered within a group of students who didn't like to ask and marks have suffered as a consequence. Similarly, do stick to what you were asked to do. It is all too easy to go off at a tangent, particularly if what you discover starts to seem more interesting than what you were asked to do.

A good approach is to break assignment tasks or essay questions into key words. These tend to fall into two categories:

1. **Content words** which indicate the subject area covered.

2. **Action words** which tell you what you are expected to do.

For example, say you were set a question such as:

   '**Analyse fluctuations in London share prices over the last ten years.**'

Here the content words are: **fluctuations, London, share prices** and **last ten years**. The topic is clearly bound both geographically and chronologically. **Analyse** is the only action word, and this indicates that you have to do more than simply report what has been happening.

Activity: Understanding action words in your assessment task

- Try to match the following action words with the appropriate meaning.
- Next check your solutions against those given at the end of this chapter.

1. Analyse	j. Describe and distinguish similarities and differences.
2. Clarify	f. Give reasons why or how; clarify, justify and illustrate.
3. Compare and contrast	h. Describe or summarise, often with an evaluation.
4. Discuss	b. Examine and break into component parts.
5. Evaluate	g. Provide a framework or explanation – usually in narrative form – of a concept, idea, event or phenomenon.

6. Explain	i. Show how things fit together; provide analogies.
7. Illustrate	e. Provide pros and cons of something; provide an opinion and justify it.
8. Justify	a. Explain, review and consider.
9. Outline	d. Provide examples; show instances.
10. Relate	l. Provide a condensed, precise list or narrative.
11. Review	c. Explain with significant detail.
12. Summarise	k. Explain why a concept can be supported, typically by using examples and other types of support.

(Adapted from Feldman, 2000: 152)

The golden rules for completing your assessment successfully are: follow the assignment brief, do just what it calls for and, if you don't understand, ask for guidance. It is as simple as that and disappointing if you waste a lot of your valuable time doing the wrong thing.

Getting feedback on your work

There are three potential sources of feedback on your assignment work:

- **self assessment**;

- **peer assessment**;

- **tutor assessment**.

Self and peer assessment can be used to obtain valuable feedback before you hand in your work. If you are very lucky your tutor may also be willing to look over a draft, but you can't expect this. For more ideas on how to obtain and use all three sources, see Chapter 7, Improving your grades through feedback from self, peer and tutor assessment.

With regard to tutor feedback, you should get written feedback on your assignment work as well as a specific mark or grade. This will give you valuable information on what you are doing right and what you need to work on. Even if you get good grades, it is important to keep taking the feedback on board if you want to progress successfully.

If you are unhappy with your grades or don't understand how the grade was arrived at, it is very useful to look at the written feedback you received. If you are still unsure, or didn't get sufficient written comments, don't be afraid to ask your tutor to go through the assessment with you.

For a detailed summary of how assessment is dealt with at your institution refer to the documentation you were given at induction. You may also find this on your institution's website or intranet.

Completing group assignments successfully

Working in and perhaps leading a group or team brings more complications and challenges through the increased complexity of interactions between people – known as **group dynamics**. When completing group assignments, there may be no formal leader and so you might have to take the lead in order to get a successful outcome.

> ### Activity: What makes a good team?
>
> Think about the qualities of a good group or team that you have been a member of and consider the following questions.
>
> - What was good about the team?
> - What areas could be improved?
> - What did you learn from the experience?

Group formation

Tuckman and Jensen (1977: 419–27, cited in Mullins, 2007: 310) suggest that groups may go through five stages, namely:

- **Forming**

- **Storming**

- **Norming**

- **Performing**

- **Adjourning**

The theory was first developed by Tuckman in a clinical environment but also seems to work well in the context of project teams, which are put together for a particular purpose and have a definite life. It is not perhaps so convincing for ongoing operations or 'business as usual' where there is a gradual turnover of staff over time, with people joining and leaving at regular intervals.

In terms of completing a group assignment we can perhaps see that the situation is very much that of a project team, which has a clear goal to complete the works by a deadline and, therefore, a fixed term of life. In the early stages, meeting, talking, organising and – perhaps most of all – bonding will all be more important than doing any of the work. Some ideas for fostering the process of group development include:

- Suggesting an early meeting to elect a leader, to look critically at the assignment brief, to discuss what has to be done, to agree who will do it and by when.

- Exchanging email addresses and mobile numbers so you can keep in touch between meetings.

- Writing down everything that was agreed and circulating it to the group by email.

- Doing something of a social nature together which is unrelated to the task, such as a quiz night or ten pin bowling, in order to help the team to bond.

- Arranging regular follow-up meetings to review progress at intervals until the deadline.

Team roles

The concept of **team roles** has been developed by Belbin (1993 and 2000). In the extensive use of **syndicated teaching** (group work) at Henley Management College, staff noticed that while some groups gelled well, others did not. Thus began the work on team roles, in an effort to explain the relative good and bad chemistry of teams. Belbin argues that while the type of behaviour evident in groups is infinite, the range of behaviours which make a useful contribution to a group is finite and these behaviours can be grouped into team roles. He draws a clear distinction between **team roles** and **functional roles**.

Activity: What are your team roles?

1. Visit http://www.belbin.com/content/page/1971/Belbin_Team_Role_descriptons.pdf and download the team role descriptors.
2. Consider which are your strongest and weakest team roles.
3. Consider how you might develop these.

When participating in group assignments it may take some time for the team to shake down into clear team roles and you may find you have a mix of team roles which is less than ideal for the task. In the latter case flexibility may be the key to getting things done and this may mean you filling gaps in your team and taking roles you would not normally choose to do. This can be a developmental experience in itself.

Leadership styles

Leading an assignment group can also be a good developmental experience and a valuable preparation for taking on leadership roles in your professional career. If you take the leadership of your group, it will be useful to consider what style you will adopt and what competences you will need.

Tannenbaum and Schmidt (1973: 162–75; 178–80, cited in Mullins, 2007: 372–4) have suggested that there are four major stages on a continuum of leadership styles ranging from boss centred to subordinate centred:

Tells ↔ **Sells** ↔ **Consults** ↔ **Joins**

Clearly at the 'tells' end of the continuum the style is dictatorial which can be effective for getting things done but can quickly alienate the team members. At the other end of the scale, 'joins' really means to abdicate leadership responsibility. In between are the ideas of selling and consulting, which have to do with gaining people's agreement and consent.

Research by consultants Hey/McBer (reported by Bloisi et al., 2007: 586–7) found that managers used six leadership styles based upon emotional intelligence competencies. They found that the best performing managers used most of them every week, depending upon the situation they encountered. The six emotional intelligence leadership styles are:

- **Coercive** – demand immediate compliance in crisis.

- **Authoritative** – mobilise employees towards a vision.

- **Affiliate** – skilled at creating emotional bonds and harmony.

- **Democratic** – build consensus through participation.

- **Pacesetting** – set high performance standards and expect self direction from others.

- **Coaching** – help others improve performance.

A useful analogy is with a golfer. Imagine a golfer who has only one club and you can perhaps see that a round of golf would be made unnecessarily difficult. With six assorted clubs in the golfer's bag the task would potentially be a lot easier. However, it's not enough to have six clubs, you also have to know when to use each of them.

Leading a group of student peers is in reality little different from leading a work team. Although the context may be different, you will find that developing your skills in the emotional intelligence competencies will make you more effective in the role and your task much easier.

Activity: Leading a team

1. Consider, if you were leading a team, what would be the likely problems and what would be the likely rewards?
2. Which leadership style(s) would you want to adopt?
3. Would the style you adopt need to be contingent upon the situation and the people involved?
4. Which emotional intelligence competencies would you need to develop and which ones do you already have?

Follow-up activities

TIME FOR ACTION – CHECKLIST

Have you:

- considered what you need to do to upgrade your learning skills?
- identified how you learn and your own learning styles?
- recognised the role of reflection in your learning?
- considered how you need to develop your critical thinking skills?
- developed your note taking, mind mapping and brainstorming skills?
- appreciated what you need to do to understand your assessments?

Further reading

Belbin, M. (1993) *Team Roles at Work*. Oxford: Butterworth Heinemann.

Belbin, M. (2000) *Beyond the Team*. Oxford: Butterworth Heinemann.

Burns, T. and Sinfield, S. (2008) *Essential Study Skills: The Complete Guide to Success at University*, 2nd edition. London: Sage.

Buzan, T. (1974) *Use Your Head*. London: BBC Books.

Buzan, T. (1995) *The Mind Map Book*. London: BBC Books.

Cameron, S. (2008) *The Business Student's Handbook*, 4th edition. Harlow: Pearson.

Cottrell, S. (2008) *The Study Skills Handbook*, 3rd edition. Basingstoke: Palgrave Macmillan.

Honey, P. (1994) *Learning Logs – A Way to Enhance Learning from Experience*. Maidenhead: Peter Honey Publications.

Jeffers, S. (1991) *Feel The Fear and Do it Anyway*. London: Arrow.

Lee-Davies, L. (2007) *Developing Work and Study Skills*. London:Thomson.

Moon, J. (1999) *Reflection in Learning and Professional Development*. London: Kogan Page.

Moon, J. (2006) *Learning Journals: A Handbook of Reflective Practice and Professional Development*, 2nd edition. Abingdon: Routledge.

Pedler, M. and Boydell, J. (1999) *Managing Yourself*. London: Lemos and Crane.

Race, P. (1995) *Who Learns Wins*. London: Penguin.

Race, P. (2007) *How to Get a Good Degree: Making the Most of your Time at University*. Buckingham: Open University Press.

Ridley, D. (2008) *The Literature Review: A Step-by-Step Guide for Students*. London: Sage.

Russell, T. (1994) *Effective Feedback Skills*. London: Kogan Page.

Websites to look up

- For further information on learning styles:

http://www.peterhoney.com/
http://www.ldu.leeds.ac.uk/ldu/sddu_multimedia/kolb/static_version.php

- For further information on reflection:

http://www.infed.org/thinkers/et-schon.htm

- For further information on critical thinking:

http://www.open.ac.uk/skillsforstudy/critical-thinking.php

- For further information on mind mapping:

http://www.mind-mapping.co.uk/
http://www.buzanworld.com/

- For further information on team roles:

http://www.belbin.com/rte.asp

Solution to understanding action words activity

1. Analyse	b. Examine and break into component parts.
2. Clarify	c. Explain with significant detail.
3. Compare and contrast	j. Describe and distinguish similarities and differences.
4. Discuss	a. Explain, review and consider.
5. Evaluate	e. Provide pros and cons of something; provide an opinion and justify it.
6. Explain	f. Give reasons why or how; clarify, justify and illustrate.
7. Illustrate	d. Provide examples; show instances.
8. Justify	k. Explain why a concept can be supported, typically by using examples and other types of support.
9. Outline	g. Provide a framework or explanation – usually in narrative form – of a concept, idea, event or phenomenon.
10. Relate	i. Show how things fit together; provide analogies.
11. Review	h. Describe or summarise, often with an evaluation.
12. Summarise	l. Provide a condensed, precise list or narrative.

Time for review and reflection

This is your space to log your reflections on this chapter, to think about what you have learnt, how you will use it and what else you need to find out.

What were the key learning points of this chapter?
What are your strengths in the areas covered by this chapter?
What areas did you identify for development?
What have you learnt about yourself?
How will you use it?
What else do you need to learn or find out about in relation to this chapter?

6 How to Plan, Conduct and Review Your Research

Overview – what's in this chapter?

- Why do you need to upgrade your research skills?
- Designing your methodology
- Using secondary source material
- What is a literature review?
- Conducting primary source research
- Developing skills for research interviews and recording the outcome
- Reviewing and evaluating your research findings
- Follow-up activities, further reading and websites to look up
- Time for review and reflection

Why do you need to upgrade your research skills?

Try completing this short self-scoring test, to assess your own level of confidence in relation to developing your research skills in order to complete your course successfully.

Activity: Why do you need to read this chapter?

You need to self score each question on a scale from 0 to 10, where 0 is low and 10 is high.

1. How much do you know about methodology?	
2. How confident would you feel about writing a research proposal?	

(Continued)

(Continued)

3. How confident do you feel about achieving academic rigour?	
4. How confident do you feel about conducting your own research?	
5. How much do you know about designing questionnaires and surveys?	
6. How confident do you feel about completing a literature review?	
7. How confident do you feel about finding and using academic sources such as books and journals?	
8. How confident do you feel about looking for other sources of data/information?	
9. How confident do you feel about using Internet sources?	
10. How confident do you feel about reviewing and evaluating your findings?	
Total score	

Interpretation

What did you score?

- Less than 50%   You definitely will find a lot of help in this chapter.
- 50%–75%   There is still plenty to learn in this chapter.
- 75%–100%   You are very confident – read on to confirm your understanding.

Whether you are writing a short essay, extended essay, dissertation or thesis, you will need to research the content, either by reading other people's work or by doing your own. These two basic categories of research sources can be explained as follows:

- **Primary source research** means finding out for yourself, at first hand. This could involve experiments, interviews, questionnaires, surveys or participant observation.

- **Secondary source research** means reading other people's work and ideas in books, journals or on websites etc.

Good research requires you to learn an appropriate range of skills and mastering these will go a long way to determining the quality of your output in terms of assessment work, together with your analytical and presentational abilities.

In this chapter we will look first at designing your methodology, together with the use of some basic research methods. Finally there are some follow-on activities, some suggested further reading, websites to look up, and some space for review and reflection.

Designing your methodology

Methodology refers to the method or methods that are to be used in order to research your work. If you are doing primary source research it is essential that you can describe your methodology before you start your research work to ensure it is **rigorous**.

Academic rigour has to do with strict adherence to normal rules or procedure both in the conduct of research and in the analysis and reporting of results. For example, interviewing only people you think might support your views, out sorting questionnaires that don't fit your contention, or ignoring lab results which produce inconvenient results are all clearly unacceptable.

Good research starts with a clear research question to be answered or a hypothesis which is to be examined. Having a good question or hypothesis will be your guiding light and will condition how you research. It is all too easy to get side-tracked and lose sight of your objective. Taking some time to refine your question or hypothesis will be important. Running your ideas past your tutor will also usually pay dividends in the long term. See also Chapter 7 on writing an extended essay, dissertation or thesis.

A **research proposal** or proposition must explain what you hope to find out, what research you will need to undertake, and how you will go about doing it – i.e. your **methodology**. You may also be required to submit a preliminary literature review. See What is a literature review section below.

In order to write your methodology, you will have to choose your research method or methods. Conducting **primary source** research will involve finding out new information for yourself and this could involve experiments, interviews, questionnaires, surveys or other methods. The key point here is that it is your data which you have collected. In contrast, **secondary source** research will require you to read other people's work and ideas in books, journals or on websites etc. Frequently your work will involve you using a combination of primary and secondary sources, with the secondary source material providing a theoretical base upon which you can interpret your own results.

Your methodology will be more convincing if you can justify the methods that you utilised in preference to other methods that you might have reasonably used. For example, you may have collected questionnaire data in preference to data from focus groups because of the difficulty of gathering individuals from remote locations together in groups.

You should also give consideration to **ethical issues** when devising and writing up your methodology. This is an area of developing importance and is to some extent related to the sensitivity of the subject area. Key questions to consider include:

- How will data be stored in order to provide for **data security**? This will include both written and electronic data which you collect.

- Will the **anonymity** of individuals be preserved in your written output, i.e. your report, essay, dissertation or thesis? In this case you will need to explain how this was achieved. For example you might state that questionnaires were completed anonymously and returned using a prepaid envelope.

- Will individuals be named in your report and, if so, to what lengths did you go to gain their **informed consent**? For example for consent to be informed, it would not be enough merely to get written permission from people that you interviewed, but rather you would need to explain how they were informed about the project and how their responses might be used.

In general, it is essential that you can describe your methodology clearly before you start researching. If you cannot do so you may waste a great deal of time exploring 'false trails' and – worse still – your results may lack sufficient academic rigour and be ultimately indefensible.

> **Activity: Defining your research question and identifying your methodology**
>
> 1. Before starting your research try to write a clear question. Then look critically at your question and ask yourself:
>
>   - Can this question be answered?
>   - What would you need to do or know to answer it?
>   - What methods could you use to investigate the question?
>   - What criticisms could be made of your methodology?
>
> 2. Now try writing up your methodology. If you can, run it past your tutor for feedback.

Conducting primary source research

As stated previously, primary source research means finding out for yourself at first hand. In certain disciplines, especially the natural sciences, this could involve experiments which may be designed or may be prescribed by your tutor.

However, in most cases it will be down to you to determine your methodology; see the section above, Designing your methodology.

Conducting **interviews** for research has the potential advantage of getting into greater depth with interviewees but the disadvantage is that the process can be time consuming, not only in terms of the time taken conducting the interviews and in travelling to locations to meet people face to face but also because of the problem of recording or transcribing notes from interviews (see the section below on skills required for interviewing and recording outcomes). **Telephone interviews** can sometimes be a compromise solution because travel time is removed and you can jot down notes as you go. However, there is always some loss of the feedback we get from reading one another's body language.

Interviews may be structured, semi-structured or free flowing and this requires another choice from the researcher. To conduct effective interviews you will need a good range of interpersonal skills. See Chapter 3 on developing your people skills, particularly the sections on questioning and listening skills and preparing for formal interviews.

Questionnaires have certain advantages over interviews as it may be possible to collect more data from more people and in a more structured way. This last point has the potential of making the data more easily analysed and reported, especially where the questions are of a quantitative nature. Even qualitative questions can be categorised and quantified. We have used coloured highlighter pens to do this, colour coding textual responses for quantitative analysis.

Because questions are prescribed in a questionnaire, it makes them inflexible when compared to a free flowing or semi-structured interview. Questions may even be misunderstood as there is no possibility of judging the response as in a face-to-face interview, where body language can be assessed and alternative or supplementary questions asked to clarify points.

When writing a questionnaire, it is easy for the designer unintentionally to embody his or her own ideas or normative assumptions. When phrasing questions it is important not to lead the respondents by asking loaded questions such as: 'Don't you think it's a bad idea that...?'. Similarly, imagine a question asking such as: 'How serious do you consider the problem of immigration to be?'. This question starts from the position that there is a problem and therefore effectively excludes anyone from responding who thinks either that it is not a problem or that immigration is a good thing. In other words it embodies a **normative assumption** of the designer.

With a 'tick box' type of questionnaire you should mix up the questions so that there is no discernable pattern to the answers which might lead the respondent to think that, say, column three was the correct answer. Even with simple questions that require only yes or no answers, there should be no chance of the respondent becoming **tick happy** or the point of the research will be lost.

In designing a questionnaire it is helpful to start by asking fairly easy questions, leaving the challenging content until later on when the respondent is more relaxed and 'warmed up'. It can also be quite useful to hide the real purpose altogether. For example if you were researching alcohol abuse, you might hide your 'real' questions among others in a general questionnaire about lifestyle. The worst idea would probably be to head it up: 'Do you have a drink problem?'.

An important decision to make will be about how your questionnaire is to be delivered to the potential respondents. Consideration must be given as to how and where data is collected. Standing around with a clip board and asking the questions yourself may produce very different results to sending out forms to be completed and returned anonymously.

A further issue with questionnaires relates to the size and composition of the **sample**, and how representative it is of the population you wish to survey. In general a larger sample might be expected to be more representative, but as a student there are also issues about how you will handle the data and you will almost certainly want to restrict the size to make it manageable.

There is also the question of which 'sample' you identify. For example, interviewing one hundred smokers would probably give you very different results from interviewing one hundred people about smoking. Both might provide interesting data, but you would need to consider this matter very carefully when designing your methodology. Again your research question should be your guiding light (see the section above on designing your methodology).

The question then arises, 'a sample of what?'. It could be of the population of a country, the staff of an organisation, or of some particular group such as fell walkers or asthma sufferers. The group being sampled must be clearly identifiable and the sample should be **representative** of it. Collecting some demographic data as part of your questionnaire – such as age, gender and ethnicity etc. – will allow you to compare the profile of your sample with that of the group it represents and in turn allow you to draw some conclusions as to just how representative it is.

A final consideration will be to **pilot** your draft questionnaires with a small sample – maybe even made up of friends – who will give you feedback on the content and construction and allow you to put things right before you start in earnest.

As with questionnaires, **surveys** are to a large extent dependant for their success upon covering a representative sample of what is being surveyed. Types of survey are many and various and include such diverse activities as counting customer footfall, i.e. people passing a site in market research, to examining aerial pictures for signs of lost buildings in archaeology.

Simple **observation** might seem to be a fairly obvious method of researching human behaviour. However, the effect of the researcher upon the research must always be acknowledged. The so-called **Hawthorne effect** refers to the tendency of people to behave differently when being observed (Mullins, 2007: 51–4). This holds implications not only for observation but also for the design of all social research methodology, in terms of the impact of researchers upon their results. For example responses to a questionnaire of a personal nature, such as illegal drug use or safer sex practice, might be quite different where the forms are returned anonymously in a plain brown envelope rather than being taken down in person by an interviewer with a clipboard.

In order to avoid problems created by the Hawthorne effect, some researchers developed **participant observation**, which required the researcher to work 'undercover'. However, this might now be considered as unethical, because of the need to gain the **informed consent** of all the participants (see earlier discussion in this chapter on Designing your methodology). **Action research** is an alternative approach, which addresses real life problems in a collaborative venture between researchers, participants and practitioners. Its success can be measured according to whether the actions solve the problems and realise change (Blumberg et al., 2005).

There are now alternative possibilities of using technology to capture what happened with microphones and even hidden cameras. However, the problem of maintaining secrecy remains and once discovered, we can expect that people will behave differently, just as drivers slow down when they see a speed camera. Use of such techniques also raises ethical issues.

Activity: Selecting your primary source methods

When you are selecting which primary source method(s) to use for your research consider the following points and questions.

- Review your assignment carefully. What are you being asked to do?
- Develop a clear research question or hypothesis to guide your work.
- Consider which method(s) would be most appropriate, most practical, and most reliable in order to complete your work successfully.

(Continued)

(Continued)

- Try to think what problems you might encounter.
- Try to foresee what criticisms might be made of your methods and how you might counter these.
- Be prepared to ask your tutor for feedback on your methodology before you commence researching.

Using secondary source material

Researching through secondary sources inevitably involves reading other people's work and ideas. Secondary sources are clearly very extensive, but can be seen to include:

- **Books** – which either may be authored or edited books of readings by other writers.

- **Academic journals** – which contain **refereed** articles, which means that submissions have passed successfully through a process of **peer review**.

- **Other journals, magazines and periodicals** – these may have useful articles but do not have the status of refereed journals.

- **Websites** – where online material can be downloaded. These require special consideration and we should ask, 'What is the source of the material and can it be trusted?'. A key question may be, 'Who is moderating the site?'.

- **Local and national government publications** – including the public record office and other sections of the National Archives, etc.

- **Organisational data** – including internal publications from companies and other organisations. These are sometimes known as **grey materials**.

Academic libraries normally hold much of the sort of secondary source material you will need, and you will usually find that your own institution's library will be geared to the needs of your course. However, if you are doing project work you may need access to other academic or specialised libraries. Local libraries can be very helpful, as for example when conducting a local history project. Similarly many organisations will have their own libraries and may welcome student researchers even if they are not open to the general public, although you may need an introduction from your own institution's library.

Visiting reader facilities allow you to use libraries which might otherwise be closed to the general public, while **inter-library loans** allow you to read work from other locations without the need to travel there, which can be a very useful and time-saving option. Your own institution's library staff should be able to advise you on such things as inter-library loans and reader facilities for other libraries.

When using secondary source materials it is all too easy to read and collect too much information and end up with a big pile of notes and no idea what to write about (see Chapter 7 on writing up your work). Be guided all the time by your research question (refer back to the section on designing your methodology). This can be used as a filter when looking for materials and when examining contents and index pages in order to make sure you read just what you need to. Using your time and energy effectively is essential if you are to achieve your goals. A good distinction here is between reading that which is: **need to know** versus **nice to know**.

When using books and journals be aware that they also provide you with other sources. You may find that the references they give you to other works are worth exploring further. Similarly websites provide you with useful links to other sites which can be explored.

Sometimes a number of works will all refer back to the same source and what you may have found here is reference to the **seminal work** – i.e. the first piece written in a particular area, often highly original and influential. Ideally we would all go back to seminal works, but that is not always a practical possibility, so be guided by your lecturers as to what to read. In many disciplines textbooks are quite acceptable and offer you a distilled account of many other works.

Activity: Identifying your secondary source material

When you are identifying secondary sources for your research consider taking the following steps.

- Ask your tutor or supervisor for any suggestions as a starting point, together with any other staff or students who have an interest in the subject area.
- Use textbooks to get an overview of the subject area, noting which sources they quote. These may be seminal works which you can go back to.
- Talk to the subject librarian at your institution's library to establish what they know or are aware of that could help you.
- Talk to specialist people at other universities or in external organisations in the field.
- Make Internet searches using academic search engines (Emerald, Google Scholar, etc.).

When you take notes from books and journals make sure that you collect all the details you will need for your bibliography (and store them carefully). For books this will include the author, year of publication of the edition you used, plus the title, edition, place of publication and publisher. Page numbers should also be noted so that you can put them in your source references and so you can find them again (see Chapter 7 on avoiding plagiarism and source referencing correctly).

When using Internet sources it is important to record the date you visited the site together with the full URL. The easiest way to capture the full URL is to cut and paste it directly into your bibliography (see Chapter 7 on source referencing correctly).

What is a literature review?

A literature review is an appraisal of the available academic work within a particular field of study. We find that students often make the mistake of simply reporting the literature rather than reviewing it. So the key word here is **review** and – depending upon what you are being asked to do – this could mean doing a combination of the following (following Blumberg et al., 2005: 154):

- Establish the context of the problem or topic by reference to previous work.

- Understand the structure of the problem.

- Relate theories and ideas to the problem.

- Identify the relative variables and relations.

- Show the reader what has been done previously.

- Show which theories have been applied to the problems.

- Show which research design and methods have been applied to the problems.

- Show which research designs and methods have been chosen.

- Rationalise the significance of the problem and the study presented, synthesise and gain a new perspective on the problem.

- Show what further work needs to be done in the light of existing knowledge.

A literature review may be an assignment in its own right, but will often be an essential component of a longer work such as an extended essay, dissertation or thesis. In this case the purpose of the literature review is to lay out the theoretical background or framework for the entire work (see also Chapter 7 on writing an extended essay, thesis or dissertation).

> ### Activity: Completing your literature review successfully
>
> 1. When you are asked to complete a literature review, take a close look at your assessment brief. What exactly are you being asked to do and why? If this is not clear, go back to your tutor and ask!
> 2. Consider which of the points in the bullet list provided above you might want to achieve in your literature review.
> 3. Try to read and take notes critically in order to extract what you need from the work in hand. You will not only need to note down quotations but also what points of analysis strike you as you read the text.
> 4. Review all your notes critically (see Chapter 5, Developing critical thinking skills), before making a plan and writing up your review.
> 5. Take a good look at your final draft. The key question for you to consider is: 'Have I provided a critical review of the literature required or simply a report of it?'.

Developing skills for research interviews and recording the outcome

As suggested earlier, one of the decisions you need to make when establishing your methodology is whether to use interviews and, if so, of what type. Interviews can be structured, i.e. based around a list of scripted questions, semi-structured or free flowing (see also Chapter 3: Questioning and listening skills, and Preparing for formal interviews). Some of the most productive interviews can be free flowing but the open format also means it is easy to miss something, so a semi-structured interview – maybe with a checklist of things to cover – can be a useful compromise.

Recording the outcome also requires some methodological decisions. There are two basic options:

- Taking notes is the obvious solution but it can seriously interrupt the flow of your interview. If you can manage with key words or a mind map, this will help immensely. You don't always need to report what people say verbatim, that is word for word; as long as you get the import of what they say it will be acceptable for most purposes.

- Using recording devices saves a lot of time in the interview but may affect your interviewees' propensity to be honest with you. It's a good idea to ask if they mind you recording the interview. Afterwards you have the problem of transcribing the recording and this can be very time consuming.

Interviewees will sometimes ask you for a copy of your notes or even a copy of the recording and this is something that may have to be discussed or even negotiated. If you are going to quote them, they might want to be sure of what they said. However, in our experience most interviewees are very helpful and forthcoming, with the right encouragement.

Reviewing and evaluating your research findings

When you have completed your research, and perhaps during the process, there comes a point when you will need to start reviewing what may be a number of disparate pieces of evidence or findings from a variety of sources. It is important to look at your own findings from primary sources as critically as you would those you read in secondary sources. See also Chapter 5, Developing critical thinking skills – especially the part on handling the intellectual argument.

Making sense of what you have found out can be a major problem and writing up your findings as you go along really helps, even if it means some extra cutting and pasting later on. If you have written up your findings it can be very useful to print off a copy at this stage to review; drawing lines, highlighting things, numbering points or whatever else helps you to review your research, before making a plan to write up your work for presentation (see Chapter 7 on writing up your work).

Both quantitative and qualitative data can be coded for efficient analysis. A simple and effective way to do this is to type responses into the columns of a spreadsheet and then to sort the data by different criteria. Where you have collected a mass of qualitative data, perhaps from questionnaires, it will be necessary to look for themes and then to categorise responses through a system of **coding**. This will ultimately allow you to report results such as 'while 87 per cent of respondents mentioned X only 12 per cent mentioned Y; however, some 6 per cent mention both X and Y'.

If there were shortcomings in your research it is better for you to draw attention to them than be criticised at assessment. Similarly, be prepared to highlight anything that you didn't or couldn't find out and why this was. It isn't always possible to do what you planned, so it is better to say so; for example an organisation can withdraw cooperation or restrict access to certain data.

Triangulation is the process of comparing results from various sources to see if they support each other. For example, you might have your own primary source data from interviews and questionnaires, plus earlier research conducted by other people that you have read in secondary sources. How do these data sets compare? Clearly if all the results are consistent it is relatively easy to draw firm conclusions with a level of certainly about the reliability of your work. If they do not, this may require explanation and perhaps further research.

Follow-up activities

TIME FOR ACTION – CHECKLIST

Have you:

- clearly identified your research question or working hypothesis?
- designed your methodology?
- written up your proposal?
- considered how you will conduct primary source research?
- identified how you will use secondary source material?
- recognised what is required for a literature review?
- developed skills for research interviews and recording the outcome?
- thought about how you will review and evaluate your research findings?

Further reading

Bell, J. (2005) *Doing Your Research, A Guide for First-Time Researchers in Education, Health and Social Science*. Maidenhead: Open University Press.

Blumberg, B., Copper, D. and Schindler, P. (2005) *Business Research Methods*. Maidenhead: McGraw-Hill.

Burns, T. and Sinfield, S. (2008) *Essential Study Skills: The Complete Guide to Success at University*, 2nd edition. London: Sage.

Cameron, S. (2008) *The Business Student's Handbook*, 4th edition. Harlow: Pearson.

Churchill, H. and Sanders, T. (2007) *Getting Your PhD: A Practical Insiders Guide*. London: Sage Publications.

Cottrell, S. (2005) *Critical Thinking Skills: Developing Effective Analysis and Argument*. Basingstoke: Palgrave Macmillan.

Cottrell, S. (2008) *The Study Skills Handbook*, 3rd edition. Basingstoke: Macmillan.

Feldman, R. (2000) *POWER Learning, Strategies for Success in College and Life*. Maidenhead: McGraw-Hill Higher Education.

Ridley, D. (2008) *The Literature Review: A Step-by-Step Guide for Students.* London: Sage.

Saunders, M., Thornhill, A. and Lewis, P (2006) *Research Methods for Business Students*, 4th edition. Harlow: Financial Times/Prentice Hall.

Walliman, N. (2004) *The Undergraduate Dissertation: The Essential Guide for Success.* London: Sage.

Websites to look up

- For further information on primary and secondary source research:

http://asp.wlv.ac.uk/Level5.asp?UserType=11&level5=5550

- For further information on developing your research methodology:

http://www.bath.ac.uk/e-learning/gold/glossary.html#glossary

- For further help with writing your literature review:

http://www.ssdd.uce.ac.uk/learner/New%20page.htm

 ## Time for review and reflection

This is your space to log your reflections on this chapter, to think about what you have learnt, how you will use it and what else you need to find out.

What were the key learning points of this chapter?
What are your strengths in the areas covered by this chapter?
What areas did you identify for development?

What have you learnt about yourself?
How will you use it?
What else do you need to learn or find out about in relation to this chapter?

7   **How to Write Up and Present Your Work in Order to Get Better Results**

Overview – what's in this chapter?

- Why do you need to upgrade your written and presentational skills?
- Writing up reports and essays
- Structuring material and constructing your arguments
- Avoiding plagiarism, source referencing and bibliographies
- Improving graphic presentation
- Improving your grades through feedback from self, peer and tutor assessment
- What else do you need to know to write an extended essay, thesis or dissertation?
- Giving effective presentations
- Follow-up activities, further reading and websites to look up
- Time for review and reflection

Why do you need to upgrade your written and presentational skills?

Try completing this short self-scoring test, to assess your own level of confidence in relation to developing your written and presentational skills in order to complete your course successfully.

Activity: Why do you need to read this chapter?

You need to self score each question on a scale from 0 to 10, where 0 is low and 10 is high.

1. How good are you at writing up essays and reports?	
2. How good are you at introducing your work?	

3. How competent are you in terms of structuring material?	
4. How confident are you about handling intellectual arguments?	
5. How good are you at summarising your arguments in your conclusions?	
6. How important are the visual aspects of presenting your work to you?	
7. How confident are you that you can source reference correctly in your reports and essays?	
8. How confident are you about writing up longer works such as extended essays, theses and dissertations?	
9. How good are you at oral presentations/public speaking?	
10. How concerned are you about improving your grades?	
Total score	

Interpretation

What did you score?

- Less than 50%   You definitely will find a lot of help in this chapter.
- 50%–75%   There is still plenty to learn in this chapter.
- 75%–100%   You are very confident – read on to confirm your understanding.

A large part of your work as a student will require you to write up work, whether it is in the form of reports, essays, dissertations or theses. The quality of your writing will go a long way to determining your grades. It is also likely that you will have to make oral presentations. These are all essential academic skills to develop if you are going to achieve your goals at university or college.

In the course of developing your skills you need to find your own voice (also discussed later in this chapter), otherwise your work is going to sound like a boring repetition of your textbooks. To do this you will need to achieve a level of confidence. Conducting good research (as outlined in Chapter 6) will help you do this, but you also have to be prepared to analyse what you have found out and to bring your own analysis and ideas into your writing. Further you will need to develop a style which is your own. In doing this, you will no doubt be influenced by what you read and by what your tutors say.

In this chapter we are going to look at written work, including some stylistic conventions for academic writing, some ideas for constructing academic arguments, and at how your work looks. We also look at avoiding plagiarism by source refer-encing correctly in the text and by constructing appropriate bibliographies or lists of references. We then look at how you can get better grades by using self, peer and tutor feedback; and the problems experienced in writing longer works such as dis-sertations and theses, together with the skills needed for giving oral presentations. Finally there are some follow-on activities, some suggested further reading, web-sites to look up, and some space for review and reflection.

Writing up reports and essays

Stylistic conventions for academic writing

When writing up academic work you will be expected to learn to follow some basic conventions. You will no doubt notice some of these when you are reading acade-mic books and articles, but the following conventions will give you some idea of what is generally considered good practice (following Cottrell, 1999: 166–7).

- **Use formal English** – academic English avoids slang and expressions such as 'These findings need to be *taken with a pinch of salt*', or 'the argument was *a bit over the top.*'

- **Avoid abbreviations and contractions** – words should be written out in full: 'didn't' as 'did not', 'dept.' as 'department', 'isn't' as 'is not'. If you feel that you have to use abbreviations such as 'OPEC' or 'ACAS', a list should be supplied at the start of the work.

- **Be impersonal** – in most disciplines they will prefer you to avoid using personal pronouns such as 'I', 'we' and 'you'. If this is the case in your discipline, you can begin sentences with phases such as:

  It can be seen that...

  There are a number of...

  It has been found that...

  However, when writing reflective statements it is quite in order to use personal pro-nouns such as 'I'. It would clearly be ridiculous to describe yourself as 'the student'.

- **Be cautious** – writers often indicate that they are aware nothing is completely certain. Insert caveats such as: perhaps, maybe, appears to, seems to, tends to, may, might, possibly, generally. These can help to protect you from criticism (see also Chapter 5, Developing critical thinking skills).

- **Avoid conjunctions** – such as starting sentences with or, and, but, or yet.

- **Be objective** – avoid subjective words such as 'nice', 'wonderful', 'natural', 'usual'.

- **Be concise** – edit out unnecessary words, for example: '...in a book called Organisational Behaviour by a man called Mullins...' can be reduced to a simple source reference (see the section below on source referencing).

- **Use continuous prose** – write in full sentences grouped together into clearly thematic paragraphs.

Writing developed introductions

How you start your report will tend to condition the reader's view of the whole piece of work, so it is important to get off to a good start. In particular your introduction should try to:

- **attract the reader's attention**. You can always start with a pertinent quotation, an interesting statistic or a question that you will try to answer.

- **explain your aims and objectives**. These relate to what you are aiming to achieve in the piece of work and how you will know that you have done this.

- **explain your methodology**. This explains how you researched your work (see Chapter 6, How to plan, conduct and review your research) and should be a separate section in a longer report, dissertation or thesis.

- **give direction to your report**. There is often a paragraph which starts 'The report will first' and then goes on, 'it will next turn to the question of...' and later says '...and finally it will...' or something similar. What you are doing here is giving the reader a short itinerary or route map to follow when reading your work (see the next section on structuring your work).

Your introduction should be more than one paragraph and should be developed into several *thematic* paragraphs. Students coming from school or college sometimes find this hard as they are used to writing only a one paragraph introduction, but it's just a case of breaking down what you have to say and developing it. For example you could follow the above bullet points, which would give you at least four paragraphs.

Developing your argument in the main body of your work

What goes between your introduction and conclusion is often referred to as the **main body** of the work or text. However, this term is never used in the work. In order to produce a cogent argument you should consider the following points.

- **Organising your content**. Organise content into a logical sequence following the directions given in your introduction (see the following section on structuring your work).

- **Writing thematically**. Organise the content thematically. In a report you can use sub-headings to help you do this.

- **Knowing what to include**. Include *need to know* and exclude *nice to know* information. Avoid waffle but explain all points clearly.

- **Avoid normative statements**. Distinguish positive and normative statements (see Chapter 5 on critical thinking).

- **Avoid unsupported arguments**. Say why and support your arguments with references to source material where appropriate (see Chapter 5 on critical thinking and below in this chapter for information on source referencing).

- **Link the parts of your work together**. Write linking sentences or paragraphs to link and connect the parts of your work. For example you might say, 'Having discussed X the report will now turn to look at Y'. Also you might want to make a brief summary of each section, which will then be collected and condensed in your 'summary conclusion'.

- **Make a logical argument**. Try to make an argument or arguments which will lead logically to your **summary conclusion**. Argue from point to point. There should never be a missing step in your analysis, nor should you jump to a conclusion which is not supported by earlier discussion, analysis and findings, etc.

Writing summary conclusions

As with your introduction, your conclusions will tend to condition your reader's view of the whole work. It is your chance to really convince the reader that you know what you are writing about, so you should aim to follow the guidance here:

- **Summarise your findings and analysis**. Go back through your report and pick out all the main points of analysis which can then be summarised in your conclusion. If it is a longer document, it might be useful to print off a draft and go through it with a highlighter pen, perhaps also jotting key words in the margin.

- **Conclude your report**. What does your analysis mean? Can you draw together all the strands and make sense of them? Have you achieved the aims and objectives you set out in your introduction – and, if not, why not?

- **Make recommendations – if appropriate**. This will depend upon the nature of your work and the discipline. For example if you are analysing a business problem-solving case study, it may be quite important to say what you think should happen next. Alternatively, if your task is to analyse two competing views of history, then clearly such a recommendation would be inappropriate.

- **Never introduce new material in your conclusion**. The reason for this is that your conclusions are the summary of your earlier analysis and as such they cannot include anything that was not part of that earlier work. While there may be a temptation to hold back some startling revelation, as in the final scene of a drama, it is not appropriate in academic work.

It can be very useful to write a preliminary conclusion before you start to write up the rest of your report. You can look at your report as taking your reader on a journey, so knowing your final destination before you start can help you to avoid taking the reader on a mystery tour and focus your writing towards the point of your conclusion.

Structuring material and constructing your arguments

When writing up your work you will need to develop a clear structure. You could start by imagining that you are taking the reader on a journey, which has a beginning, a middle and an end. The beginning is your introduction, the middle or main body is your findings and discussion, and the end is your conclusion. The more clearly you can explain that journey, the more likely it is that the reader will engage with your work.

An essay can be described as a short intellectual discussion. Typically you will not use sub-headings, but will be expected to introduce your essay, discuss the topic or essay question, and then bring your work to a justified conclusion. Your conclusion should follow from your analysis and answer the question you posed in the introduction. You will also be expected to use source references throughout the essay and to provide a corresponding bibliography or list of references.

A formal report will tend to look different to an essay but will again require you to make an intellectual argument, but within a more rigid formant. A formal report will typically be structured as follows:

- Title page.

- Contents page.

- List of any abbreviations and any acknowledgements (if appropriate).

- A well-developed introduction, i.e. more than just one paragraph.

- Methodology – which will form part of your introduction in shorter reports.

- Findings and analysis reported under appropriate sub-headings.

- Well-developed summary conclusions and perhaps recommendations if appropriate.

- A full bibliography or list of references.

- Any relevant appendices.

If you have collected a lot of material it can be quite difficult to construct a cogent essay or report. In fact a large pile of notes can seem quite intimidating. The problems include what to mention and what to leave out and how to structure the content so as to reach your conclusion. It can really help to adopt the following systematic approach:

- Start by reviewing all your notes, page by page, making a mind map to identify key points/headings that you might want to include (see Chapter 5 on mind mapping).

- Now review your mind map and highlight those points you really want in your work. Exclude anything which is peripheral or tangential.

- Then number points or headings in a logical sequence that makes sense to you. Be prepared to change the sequence until you are happy with it.

- Next number your notes from your mind map, in the left-hand margin and perhaps using a different colour for each reference number.

- Open a computer file and enter your headings or key points from your mind map in first.

- Now you can write around headings or key points, inserting quotations or points where appropriate from your notes. It is useful to tick off points as you include them to avoid using the same one twice in the same piece of work.

- Use 'cut and paste' if necessary, to revise your sequence.

- Use 'word count' regularly to check length. This will help you achieve something close to the required word length.

On this last point, writing to the required length is a skill with which many students struggle. We find many students worry about not being able to write enough, but also that many students actually overshoot the total – perhaps as a result of worrying about not writing enough. Here are a few more tips that might help you avoid this:

- Take your essay or report plan and try to estimate how many words there might be in each section. Then you can check your word count, by section, as you write. You might find it doesn't quite work out how you planned but at least you have a chance to adjust as you go along.

- If you undershoot, try to look back and expand on what you wrote, adding anything you missed and explaining things in more detail.

- If you overshoot look through and try to edit out anything which is unnecessary to your argument. One trick is to take content which is relevant but not vital and make it into an appendix that can then be referred to in the report.

Activity: Structuring your written work

- Try making a mind map to help you structure your next piece of work.
- Use the systematic approach outlined in this section to structure your work.
- When you have completed your work, think about how useful you found this approach and what you have learnt.

In writing up reports and essays, you should also try to develop your own **voice**. This is that part of what you write which is in your own words and may also embody your own thoughts. The balance between your voice and citation of other people's work will depend both upon the academic discipline within which you are writing and also the assessment you are completing.

Similarly the use of **personal pronouns** such as 'I' and 'my' will be looked upon very differently in different disciplines. As suggested earlier in this chapter, the tendency in academic work is towards the impersonal, but you should be guided by your tutors on this point.

Avoiding plagiarism, source referencing and bibliographies

What is plagiarism and how to avoid it?

Plagiarism is the act of copying the words, the ideas or even the structure of the work of another writer or writers, without giving them due credit. It is seen as an act of dishonesty or intellectual theft and cases of plagiarism are taken very seriously in higher education. If your work is found to include copied work, including cut and pasted elements from the Internet, you will be penalised and your work could be awarded zero. You may also face disciplinary action and might even be asked to leave your institution.

The good news is that you can copy as much of other people's work as you want provided that you give them due credit by citing your sources. In order to do this correctly and to avoid committing acts of plagiarism it is important to adopt a recognised system of source referencing for all quotations and ideas drawn from your reading.

Activity: What does your institution say about plagiarism?

Review the materials that you were supplied with as part of your induction and also search for anything relevant to plagiarism on your institution's website. In particular try to find out:

- What do they say about plagiarism?
- What penalties might plagiarism incur?
- What can you do to avoid this?
- Is there a recommended or preferred system of source referencing?

There are various systems for source referencing, and you should be guided by your institution as to which you should use, for while some have adopted a particular system others are more liberal. The two basic systems are:

- **Harvard Convention** – this involves you inserting limited details in the text of your report, so as the reader can trace the full details of each source in your **reference list/bibliography**, which is an alphabetical list by author of books and other sources that you have used. Sometimes this is divided into two separate lists: a list of **references** used in the text and a **bibliography** of other relevant material you may have looked at.

- **Reference numbers** – this requires you to place a unique reference number against each quotation or citation in the text of your report, which can then be traced by the reader to a single numerical list of **references**.

In each case the system should be operated in such a way as to allow the reader to trace the source from the text back to the original work, creating something akin to what accountants call an 'audit trail'.

If you make an honest but incorrect attempt to source reference correctly, this will not be considered as plagiarism. However, you may find that you lose marks, so it's a good idea to learn the skills you are going to need as soon as possible after starting your course and before you submit your first piece of work.

A colleague told us...

A senior colleague told us that he had attended an American university. Having worked hard on his first piece of work, he was surprised to find that he had been awarded zero per cent! Upon enquiring he was told that he had failed to reference his sources. He never made that mistake again and went on to have a long and successful academic career.

Making Harvard Convention citations in your text

In the Harvard Convention, citations in the text for references drawn from books you have used are made using the author's surname, followed by the year of the publication and page number or numbers. For example, if you are using the author's name in the sentence it would appear like this:

According to Lee-Davies (2007: p.54) "............"

If you are not mentioning the author's name in your discussion then it can go inside the brackets like this:

(Bratten et al., 2007: pp.127–8)

Notice in the above example that a range of pages has been referred to, rather than a single page. This can be particularly useful when referring to or paraphrasing an idea or concept rather than a quotation. However, a quotation may also go over more than one page.

Where writers have more than one publication in the same year, then a suffix letter is placed after the year, both in the text, as shown in the following example, and in the bibliography or list of references.

(Entwistle and Marton, 1984a: p.47)

There are extra considerations when referencing a source that is quoted in another work, as for example where you use a core textbook which enables you to read about a variety of ideas and concepts from many authors in one book. If you are citing a work from another writer, you need to give the details of both works and to add the words 'cited in', as shown in the following two examples

Belbin (1993: p.23, cited in Mullins, 2007: p.332)

(Belbin, 1993: p.23, cited in Mullins, 2007: p.332)

When citing an Internet publication, you can give the 'stem' of the URL and the year of the material if available, or the date accessed in the text. For example:

(delni.gov.uk, 2007)

Activity: Inserting a Harvard citation in the text

1. Write a sentence in this box, including a 'Harvard' citation, drawn from your notes, which might appear in your work.

2. Check that the style is consistent with the examples we have given.

Making a Harvard Convention list of references/bibliography

If using the Harvard Convention your work should include a list of references and/or a bibliography. You should only list books, journals, pamphlets, Internet sources, etc. that you have used. A list of references/bibliography should be an alphabetical list by author/editor generally, where the format for entries is as explained in the following examples.

For books you should give the author, year, title (in italics or underlined), edition (if not first), place of publication and publisher. For example:

> Cottrell, S. (2003) *The Study Skills Handbook*, 2nd edn. Basingstoke: Palgrave Macmillan.

If you have a 'cited in' reference, as in the example given earlier, then the entry will follow the style in this example:

> Belbin, R. M. (1993) *Team Roles at Work*. Oxford: Butterworth, cited in Mullins, L. J. (2007) *Management and Organisational Behaviour*, 8th edn. Harlow: Pearson.

For journals you should give the author, year, title of article (in inverted commas), together with the journal title (in italics or underlined), volume and page numbers (beginning and ending). For example:

> Brewster, C. (2007) 'Comparative HRM: European views and perspectives', *The International Journal of Human Resource Management*, Vol. 18, pp.769–87.

Material published on the World Wide Web will often be available in print, in which case the normal reference format can be adopted. If not, ensure that the URL for the source of the document is provided, together with the title of the site and the date visited. For example:

> **Department for Employment and Learning Research Agenda 2007–9 [online]. Available from: http://www.delni.gov.uk/researchagenda0709final.pdf [Accessed 27 June 2007]**

While we normally cite published sources in our work which can be traced back to their source, there may be times when other so-called **grey list** literature might be acceptable. For example, if you were researching absenteeism at a particular company as part of a module in Human Resource Management, you might want to cite the company's internal procedures which had been issued to staff as a pamphlet. However, it is increasing likely that you will find this type of material on the company website, which offers an alternative method of citation as an Internet source.

Activity: Making a Harvard reference in your reference list or bibliography

1. Make a reference list/bibliography entry in this box, which refers to the 'Harvard' reference you cited in the previous activity.

2. Check that the style is consistent with the examples we have given.

Bibliography/reference list format

When constructing a list of references/bibliography, your task can be made much easier by inserting the entries electronically into a table. This allows you to add entries from time to time, when you are researching your work, as and when the information becomes available. Then before you complete your work you can sort the entries alphabetically, which potentially will be much quicker and more accurate than doing this manually.

This concludes a brief description of Harvard Convention referencing system, which we believe is the easiest system to use. However, you may prefer or be required to use the alternative reference number system.

Using the reference number system of referencing

The main alternative to using the Harvard Convention is to adopt a system of reference numbers. This involves inserting sequential numbers, from one onwards, against all your references to source material in the text of your work. Thus a reference might appear as follows:

According to Moon[1] **"..........."**

Where there is no mention of the author's name, as for example where quoting statistics, the number might simply appear after the source material:

The 2006/07 annual report also shows a decrease in the number of claims to employment tribunals with 105,177 cases compared to 109,712 in 2005/06[2]

Making a list of references

Your list of references will be similar to that of a Harvard Convention list of references or bibliography, except that you must list all your sources against numbers from one onwards, as for example:

1. Moon, J. (1999) *Reflection in Learning and Professional Development*. London: Kogan Page.

2. ACAS [online]. Available from: http://www.acas.org.uk/index.aspx?articleid=1312 [Accessed 5 September 2007].

If you have a further reference from the same work on the next line of your list you can use the abbreviation **ibid**., meaning 'as previously'. This would appear as follows:

3. Ibid.

If you have made further citations to a work listed earlier in your list of references, you can use the abbreviation **op. cit.**, meaning 'in a work already cited'. This might appear as follows:

7. Moon, J. (1999), op. cit.

Harvard or reference numbers?

While the reference number system is somewhat easier to explain than the Harvard system. Here are some of the advantages of each as we see it:

Advantages of Harvard Convention	Advantages of Reference Numbers
You get some limited details in the text which might obviate the need to always consult the list of references or bibliography.	You only have to put a number in the text, so less information to clutter it up and interfere with the flow.
You only need to list sources once in the list of references or bibliography, no matter how many times you cite them.	You can see sequentially how all the sources appear in the text.
You can trace sources alphabetically in your list of references or bibliography.	You can trace sources numerically in your list of references.

Including sources not cited in your text

One question that arises with both systems is, 'what if I consulted sources but did not cite them in the text?'. There is a strong argument for listing these, first because it shows the breadth of your reading and secondly because they may have influenced your thinking without you realising it. If so you will have a partial defence against any claim of plagiarism. In both systems it is easy enough to include additional sources in a separate bibliography, after your list of references.

Improving graphic presentation

Your academic work will not only be judged by its intellectual content, but also by how it looks. Good layout gives your work visual impact. A key question here is, how attractive does your report look before you start reading the content? Some key points to consider here are:

- **Title page** – this will normally be the first thing the reader sees. It should be well laid out and as a minimum should include your report title, name, course, and perhaps seminar group and word count.

- **Contents page** – this should list all the sections, sub-sections and appendices, which should be *left justified*, with page numbers on the right-hand side. If you are unsure, please refer to the format of the contents page of this book.

- **Sub-headings** – these should be used throughout the body of your report, including your introduction and conclusion. Sub-headings should be thematic, indicating to the reader the content of the sub-section.

- **Paragraph formation** – link sentences into clear paragraphs. Consider linking very short paragraphs and breaking longer ones up.

- **Spacing** – sections and paragraphs should be spaced consistently throughout your report. Good use of space gives your report visual impact and appeal – it looks good.

- **Widows and orphans** – try to avoid both 'widows' (where an odd word or line, often part of a sub-heading, appears at the top of a page) and 'orphans' (where the first line of a paragraph is left separated at the bottom of a page). Space the text over the pages so as to link it together.

- **Font sizes** – keep these consistent throughout your report, although you can use different font sizes for headings to good graphic effect.

- **Source references, bibliography or list of references** – use the correct format advised by your institution and/or tutors. See also the section above on avoiding plagiarism and source referencing correctly.

- **Appendices** – these should be identified by a number or letter in the top right-hand corner. They will always be the last part of your report or portfolio.

Activity: Improving the graphic impact of your work

- Review the bullet list above and then note down anything that you need to do from it to improve your graphic presentation skills.

- Spend some time looking over your next piece of work, asking yourself how it looks and whether you have taken all the points you identified on board?

Improving your grades through feedback from self, peer and tutor assessment

Self assessment

You can significantly improve your chances of getting good grades by taking a little time to check over your work. The most widely used definition of self assessment has been provided by Boud (1986: 1),

> Self-Assessment involves students taking responsibility for monitoring and making judgements about aspects of their own learning.

To make the self-assessment process really effective you can use a systematic approach. The self-assessment sheet included in the next activity was compiled after we recorded the errors made by over 100 undergraduates submitting work for tutor assessment. The idea is that if you self assess your own work and correct as many errors as possible before handing in, then you can avoid losing marks in those areas.

Activity: Self assessing your work to improve your grades

Try using this tick sheet to self assess your work before handing it in.

Have you: **Tick**

In general

- Followed the assignment brief you were given in completing your work?   ☐
- Completed all the tasks that were set?   ☐

Construction

- Given your work a title and created a title page?   ☐
- Created a contents page showing page numbers on the right-hand side?   ☐
- Written a well-developed introduction?   ☐
- Used sub-headings to group your ideas thematically within the main   ☐
  body of your report?
- Written a well-developed summary conclusion and remembered not   ☐
  to introduce new material in it?
- Given attention to the visual presentation including fonts, font sizes,   ☐
  spacing and layout?
- Submitted other documents required as appendices to your report?   ☐

Intellectual argument

- Avoided normative statements that do not offer any evidence?   ☐
- Supported positive statements with examples drawn from your   ☐
  experience or evidence from your reading?
- Provided clear and logical arguments?   ☐
- Structured your arguments so as to reach your conclusion?   ☐

Source material

- Used appropriate source material (books, journals, etc.) to support   ☐
  your arguments?
- Used an acceptable system of source referencing in the text of your work? ☐
- Ensured that all references in your text can be traced directly to your   ☐
  bibliography or list of references?

(Continued)

(Continued)

Submission

- Put your name on your work?   ☐
- Included all that was asked for?   ☐
- Submitted your work within the deadline set?   ☐

Your comments on your work

What were your strengths in completing the work and what areas for development did you identify?

Your self–assessed grade

What degree classification, grade or percentage do you think your work deserves?

Review of self assessment

How useful did you find the self-assessment process?

Some of the advantages of self assessment can be seen to include the following.

- It is a developmental experience for you in terms of learning to be reflective, self-critical, constructive, and to learn from the experience in order to inform future practice.

- To engage you more fully in the assessment process rather than being a passive recipient of it. To help you see yourself as an 'active partner' in the assessment processes.

- To encourage a climate of self-criticism in which you might perhaps be both more open to and less reliant upon the feedback you receive from your tutors.

- To help you develop realistic expectations about your work, and thus to help avoid surprise and/or disappointment with final marks, grades or comments.

 A student told us...

A final year student told us that he had photocopied a stack of our self-assessment sheets in year one and then used them in all his modules throughout his course. By doing this he had picked up a lot of errors and was convinced that he had increased his overall marks.

Peer assessment

> Peer assessment can be defined as an arrangement for peers to consider the level, value, worth, quality or successfulness of the products or outcomes of learning of others of similar status. (Topping et al., 2000: 149)

In addition to self assessing your own work it can be very useful to get someone else – a peer – to look over your work and to give you feedback. Your peer can use the same categories as used in the previous self-assessment activity. However, it is important not to take comments on board if you don't agree with them because, in the end, it has to be your work.

Tutor assessment

The ultimate assessment of your work will probably be by your tutor. We know that the most important thing for most of our students is the grade awarded, but we would ask you to look carefully at the comments your tutors have made, which may ultimately be the most valuable feedback that you get.

Taking some time to work though the comments, trying to work out what you did well and where there is room for improvement, will help you to grow and develop in your course and beyond. If you don't understand or agree with the comments you should find a time and place to discuss them with your tutor; tutors are usually happy to do this.

What else do you need to know to write an extended essay, thesis or dissertation?

At some time in your course it is likely that you will have to write an extended essay, dissertation or thesis. Many students panic at the thought of writing five, ten, fifteen or perhaps twenty thousand words, but we find that far more students overshoot the word count than undershoot it.

In order to complete your longer pieces of work successfully there are number of areas to consider:

- **Topic** – finding something to explore, designing a research question, setting aims and objectives, and also setting parameters for your study.

- **Timescale** – establishing a time plan in order to complete your work by the deadline.

- **Methodology** – deciding how you will go about researching.

- **Literature review and/or theoretical framework** – critically reviewing existing literature and creating a theoretical framework for your work.

- **Reporting and analysing your findings** – developing your analysis into a cogent argument which leads logically to your conclusions.

- **Conclusions** – summarising your analysis, concluding your work and answering the question which you set or explaining why you couldn't do so.

- **Format** – making sure that you adopt an acceptable format to report your work including citation and source referencing.

However, the good news is that what you will have learnt about writing shorter essays and reports applies to longer works too.

Finding a topic to explore

You will probably have to select your own topic, probably agreeing a research question or outline with your tutor or supervisor at an early stage. The key question here is: is the project doable? You may have a brilliant idea, but if it would take a team of skilled researchers five years working flat out to complete, forget it.

The most common problem we find is that students pick too big a topic, perhaps because they fear not having enough to write about. They then find it too big and unmanageable, both to research and write up.

> **Activity: What am I going to research for my extended essay, dissertation or thesis?**
>
> - Take some time out to think about what you would like to research. It is useful to look back over your course notes. What interested you and what would you like to know more about?
> - Try making a mind map (see Chapter 5 on mind mapping) to explore what you know already about your potential topic and what you think you might research.
> - Try writing a 'research question', stating in one sentence what you hope to find out or explore. Time spent refining your question will help you to focus both your research and your writing.
> - Ask critically whether the project is doable and, if you think it is, try running it past your tutor or supervisor.

It's very useful to reduce your ideas to a single research question which states succinctly what you are trying to find out. Time spent refining and developing this question can pay great dividends over the life of your project. If you can't write a clear research question, then your ideas are still unfocused and you are likely to spend a lot of time collecting too much material. You are also likely to have problems writing up your research and reaching a clear conclusion.

Setting parameters or limitations for your research is an essential step if your project is not going to grow too large and become unachievable. It's a question of narrowing down your work to manageable proportions to keep it doable. For example parameters could include research into:

- **a particular topic**, such as 'a study into absenteeism among train drivers working on the London Underground System'.

- **a geographical area** such as 'a study of low pay among seasonal employees in Cardiff'.

- **a historical period** e.g. the development of British Government policies promoting the development of the welfare state between 1945 and 1948.

Setting aims and objectives can further help to clarify what you want to get out of the project. Students sometimes get confused about the difference between the two. The distinction is simply that aims are about what you expect to do whereas objectives are about outcomes that can be measured. A good analogy can be drawn with archery, where you take aim before you release your arrows. You aim to hit the very centre of the target, but only later inspection of it will tell you whether you achieved your objective or not.

Activity: Establishing aims, objectives and parameters

In terms of your research question, try to establish:

- clear parameters for your study.
- aims which you hope to achieve.
- objectives against which you can assess your success in achieving your aims.

Establishing your timescale

Many students find that having a lot to do and being given a long timescale to do it in is a real problem. Effective time management will be essential to completing your work on time and to the standard you want to achieve (see also Chapter 4, Managing your time). Some good rules for completing longer works include:

- **Start early**. You might have got away with last minute panics on reports and essays in the past, but a longer work will definitely find you out. Trust us, you won't write 20,000 words on the night before the deadline!

- **Break down the task**. Breaking the work into manageable chunks means that you don't have to face something that feels akin to climbing Everest, but rather a series of small and manageable uphill steps.

- **Make a time plan**. Making a time plan which gives a deadline for completing each step or stage can really help you manage your time. It's no good having just one deadline – i.e. the hand-in date – you need a series of mini-deadlines along the way.

- **Write up as you go**. There is no reason why you can't open files on day one and then start to write up material as you gather it from your research – and even record your thoughts as you go. It can either be cut and pasted into the final document or deleted if not required. Similarly, you can start building your reference list or bibliography right from the start, entering each source as you find it.

- **Don't wait to start writing up until you have got all your research done**. If you wait till you have everything you will never start, because there is always something else to find out. It is quite acceptable to leave some questions unanswered, as long as you make this clear in your conclusions.

Format

In terms of the format, you should get guidance as to what is required of you from your tutors, but typically the work will break down into sections such as:

- An executive summary or abstract – this provides a short overview of the whole work.

- A well developed introduction which will introduce the work, explain why you are doing it and what you hope to find out. It may also include your research question, your aims or objectives together with the scope of the project. The scope is important in drawing lines around the project to mark out its extent. For instance you might be researching something between certain dates or within a geographical area.

- A theoretical chapter or literature review in which you critically review existing literature within the field of study. (See Chapter 6 on secondary source research and literature reviews).

- Your methodology, which describes how you will research the project (see Chapter 6 on designing your methodology).

- A report and analysis of your findings and/or data. This may be more than one chapter, especially in a longer dissertation or thesis.

- A conclusion and perhaps recommendations, which bring together all the earlier analysis in your work.

- A bibliography and/or list of references. See also section above on avoiding plagiarism and source referencing correctly.

- Any appendices. A good rule with appendices is to include only what is relevant and useful to the reader, not everything you collected during the life of the project. Remember it is an academic work and not a scrap book.

Developing your analysis

Make sure you report your findings systematically, step by step, in order to build a picture that can be summarised in your conclusions. In a longer piece of work you may find it useful to make a summary at the end of each chapter or section. Your final conclusions will then summarise the earlier summaries.

It is important to link your findings back to your literature review or theoretical framework, remembering that while they might be separate sections, they are not unrelated. We see too many dissertations where the literature is 'hermetically sealed' within the literature review section rather than forming a theoretical framework for the entire work.

You can be kind to your reader by telling a consistent story which makes sense as a whole, rather than by writing a series of discrete sections which don't link together. Try to take your reader on a journey from your introduction to your conclusion – one which they can understand. Link one section to another with linking paragraphs and phrases (see also the section above on writing up reports and essays). It is very hard to appreciate what a work is all about if you have to keep reading and re-reading it in order to see how it fits together.

Developing your conclusions

Remember that your conclusions are essentially a summary of earlier analysis and so you should never introduce anything new. Summarising longer pieces of work is a skill in itself. A good tip is to print off a draft and then to highlight all the key points of analysis you want to summarise. Your sections or chapters may already contain discrete summaries, as suggested earlier, which can be brought together in your final conclusions.

Make sure that your conclusions either answer the research question that you set out to answer, and the aims and objectives that you established, or explains why they do not. Your objectives should be your measure of what you achieved. It is quite acceptable to highlight any unanswered questions, areas you could not complete or explore fully, and to suggest these as subjects for further research. If you didn't find what you expected, you may need to change the initial question, aims and objectives, your abstract or executive summary and your introduction. This may need to be negotiated with your academic supervisor.

It is good to be humble in your work and especially your conclusions. It is far better to say 'from the limited scope of the research, the evidence would seem to suggest that...' rather than 'it has been proven conclusively that...'. In academic work, to be overly bold is to lay yourself open to criticism. See also Chapter 5 on developing critical thinking for further discussion.

Giving effective presentations

Why do we need to develop our presentational skills?

As part of your course, it is very likely that you will have to present some of your work orally. The formal presentation has many purposes beyond your education including internal corporate briefings, the sales pitch to customers and the public relations address. In each case we are seeking to inform and influence, and in doing this we are primarily selling ourselves. If people believe in us, they will probably believe in our message.

If you have a presentation to deliver, you will need to think about what you want to say, who you want to say it to, and how. Knowing and understanding your message is clearly an essential starting point.

> ### Activity: Thinking about your experiences of presentations
>
> Take a few minutes to think about the following questions.
>
> - What have been your good and bad experiences of hearing other people make a presentation?
> - What are your own good and bad experiences of making a presentation?
> - What have you learnt from these experiences?

The audience

The first question to consider is, who are you trying to get your message across to? If you have the power to invite who you want to your presentation, then obviously some thought will have to be given to the guest list. Try inviting some people who might be expected to agree with you or who are generally receptive to new ideas, to help the balance of the audience. Think about how you invite them, what documentation you send out in advance, and what you ask them to do or prepare in anticipation.

If your audience is predetermined, try to find out what you can in advance by asking:

- What do they need to know?

- What do they know already?

This will help you to pace and pitch your presentation, neither insulting their intelligence nor assuming too much prior knowledge. If you are unsure, start with basics and build up your argument. It is wise to avoid technical terms and jargon which they don't understand – if it is necessary, explain the meanings.

> ### Activity: Identifying the audience
>
> If you are planning a presentation, take a few minutes to consider the following issues.
>
> - Who are your audience?
> - What do they need to know?
> - What will you expect them to know already?

Identifying and structuring content

Decide what you want to say and how you think you may say it to your audience. **Brainstorming** techniques (see Chapter 5 on mind mapping and brainstorming) are useful for working out what could be said, but be beware of overloading your audience and losing your message in a morass of detail.

Try to distinguish 'need to know' from 'nice to know' information and identify the key points you want to get across. Arrange key points in a logical sequence which makes sense. Points should follow on clearly from one to another. Try to start at a point with which people are already familiar and then draw linkages between points to create a thread which runs through your presentation.

Everybody in the audience will have a natural **attention span** after which they will tend to turn off and go into 'private circuits'. Remember looking out of the window at school! We can, however, extend attention span by the use of good presentational techniques.

Three is considered by some to be a 'magic' number in presentational skills. Our suggestion is:

- Don't expect to get more than three major points across in one presentation.

- Be prepared to repeat them all three times.

Sadly, people will forget most of what you say, however well you say it, so remembering the **magic three** can really help you to limit what you say and also to reinforce it by repetition.

Thinking about how you start

Entertainers talk about 'winning an audience', and a strong introduction will make this task much easier while a poor one can make it impossible. You should, therefore, try to do three things:

- Get the audience's attention.

- Introduce yourself to them.

- Introduce your message and how you will deliver it.

Thinking about how you finish

Your conclusion is similarly important. Try to leave your audience on a positive note. Thank them for coming and for their attention, and ensure that you repeat and reinforce the key points of your message.

An old maxim is: 'Tell them what you are going to tell them, tell them, and then tell them what you told them' – that is introduction, body and conclusion. Again, it is the **magic three**!

Oral delivery

Your voice will be your most important piece of equipment when making a presentation and it deserves some consideration. The way we use our voices can be decisive in winning over our audience and getting our message across. We have the power to inspire people or send them to sleep!

If you were preparing to play sports you might reasonably expect that you would have to do some training. Similarly, singers and actors have to work hard to develop their voices. For some reason people who have to speak in public usually expect that it will just happen. A little work and practice in this area, however, can pay great dividends. Some key ideas for improving your vocal projection include:

- **Breathe!** Learning to regulate your breathing is the most vital presentational skill. Like singers and actors, we should aim to breathe deeply from the abdomen in order to give us power and control over our voices. Breathe deeply to give yourself the power you need to present.

- **Practice** breathing slowly and regularly before you speak and it will help you to calm your nerves.

- **Volume** – aim to fill the room, reaching the furthest in your audience without blasting out those closest to you. Changes of volume can be very effective in making a key point, drawing the audience in by lowering your voice and reinforcing by raising it.

- **Pace your delivery** – too slow and you will bore them, too quick and you will lose them. Aim for a comfortable pace, but if you are nervous, slow down a little to avoid the natural tendency to speed up.

- **Pitch your voice** at a level which is comfortable to you. Again, if you are nervous, pitch down a little to avoid the natural tendency for it to rise.

- **Tone** – warm and friendly is usually best, but other tones may be appropriate in particular situations. Aggressive tones usually lead to further aggression and may risk alienating your audience.

- **Vary pace, pitch and tone** to accentuate points.

- **Drink water!** Make sure you drink plenty of water to avoid getting too dry and have some with you when presenting. It can be thirsty work!

- **Warm up your voice** beforehand if you can. Chatting with people will help.

Activity: Projecting your voice

If you have difficulty in speaking up and/or projecting your voice, this exercise will help you develop a stronger voice for presentations. Try doing this every day until your next presentation.

1. Place one hand on your chest and the other on your abdomen. Feel and be very sensitive to your breathing.
2. Start breathing more slowly and more deeply and be very aware that your abdomen should now be moving in and out, far more than your chest.
3. Repeat your name, at first in your normal speaking voice and then a little louder each time until you have filled the room.
4. Make a note each day of how it went. You can score your own voice on a scale of 0 to 10, where 0 equals silence and 10 is enough to fill the room where you have to give a presentation.

Body language

We can use body language to good effect if we stop repressing it. We shouldn't fear using facial expressions, hand and arm movements, etc. to reinforce our message.

It helps to start with a smile. Try looking around and smiling at everybody before you say your first word. It is also good to keep moving. Standing, sitting and walking around at different points in the presentation can help break it up and extend attention spans.

Maintain eye contact with your audience, looking around the room to keep everybody involved and watching for those drifting off into 'private circuits'. To do this you will need to learn to speak from headings rather than a script. This becomes easier once you get over the fear of drying up! If you are well prepared this is unlikely to happen.

Audio-visual aids

Your message may be enhanced by the use of appropriate audio-visual aids, so it is worth considering where you can show something more clearly than you can describe it. Methods include: overhead projectors including OHP slides, Powerpoint and other computer-linked presentations, film and slide projectors, videos, closed-circuit television, maps, charts, posters, graphs and pre-prepared flip charts.

A good rule is never to use technical equipment you don't feel confident with. Many a presentation has been undermined by someone learning on the job! If possible, practice with the equipment beforehand, so you can feel confident on the day. Although often very busy, technicians can also be very helpful in showing you how to work equipment, particularly if you approach them politely and well before your presentation.

Handout materials

Handouts can be useful but please keep in mind that most will be either filed or thrown away, that few will actually be read, and that too many handouts can also be intimidating. Starting a presentation with a handout can also divert attention from the speaker or visual aids, so it is worth considering if and when you give them out.

Venue and layout

Not every venue is suitable for the presentation we are planning to give. Try to minimise problems by checking them out in advance, and arriving early on the day. Audio-visual aids need to be ordered, confirmed, and checked before use. Even a simple white board quickly becomes useless without the correct pens and a suitable wiper!

Tables and desks, particularly in rows, form a barrier and a friendly circle or 'horseshoe' format may well work better for your purposes. Don't be afraid to rearrange the furniture into a friendlier format.

Dealing with problems

Getting started on time involves being assertive, raising your voice if necessary and 'stewarding' people if they won't sit down.

Giving an overview, being clear about what is going to happen and how long it will take helps to avoid some problems later on. Make clear your policy on questions, for example by saying early on either 'please feel free to stop me…' or 'all questions at the end please'.

Building rapport with the audience will help to minimise problems. You can use the tone of your voice, which can be both warm and reassuring, together with your body language – perhaps giving a smile or a nod as and when appropriate. You can also ask questions of the audience to help engage people.

Interruptions require a decision, either to allow or to postpone. Techniques for dealing with interruptions include:

- **Reframing** – difficult questions can be reframed, for example by asking 'so what do other people think about that?'.

- **Reflection** – some questions can be 'reflected', i.e. repeated back to the questioner. You might say for example, 'That's a good question, but what would you want to say about it?'.

- **Deflection** – some questions cannot be dealt with on the spot, so you might say, 'Could we talk about that after the session?', or 'If you could drop me a line, I can look into that for you'.

However, it is not good to avoid questions, or to alter your vocal tone or body language as this will look defensive.

Overcoming anxiety

We know that many people get very anxious about making presentations but also that this will diminish over time if you learn to control your anxiety (see Chapter 4, Handling stress and developing relaxation techniques). Avoidance of presentations will always bring greater anxiety.

A student told us...

A student told us that he was so nervous that he couldn't do a five minute presentation that was a required part of his course and that he was considering dropping out altogether. We persuaded him to stand up and do just one minute. After ten minutes we had to stop him, although he was only half way through what he had prepared! He had no idea where the time had gone, having forgotten all about his nerves once he got started.

Reconceptualisation involves changing what you think about something. Identifying positive thoughts and focusing on these can be a positive step in reconceptualisation. **Affirmations** are statements that we choose to repeat in order to help us reconceptualise. For example: '**I am always calm and relaxed when giving a presentation**'. There are three points to bear in mind when formulating your own affirmations:

- An affirmation is always a lie if we need to say it. When we don't, it is redundant!

- Affirmations should normally start with 'I' and should always be personal to ourselves – so they should never start with 'you' or 'we'.

- Affirmations should be positive and avoid negatives. For example 'I will speak confidently' rather than 'I won't be nervous'.

Activity: Using affirmations to help overcome anxiety

1. Score your level of anxiety about making presentations.
2. Identify three positive affirmations about making presentations.
3. Repeat your affirmations at least twenty times a day.
4. After your next presentation, re-score your level of anxiety about making presentations.

Some top tips for overcoming presentation anxiety are:

- Prepare your presentation thoroughly, using the techniques outlined in this section. It may sound obvious, but knowing what you are talking about is a big confidence booster and not knowing can be truly terrifying.

- Practise your breathing and vocal projection at least once a day using the exercise in the Projecting your voice activity above. As you voice gets stronger you will also feel more confident.

- Use affirmations to change the way you think (see previous activity).

- Visualise yourself being confident when you present your work (see Chapter 2, Visualising your success).

- Practise your presentational skills as often as you can, with or without an audience. Repetition will bring confidence in your own ability.

Improving your presentational skills through feedback

Just as with your written work, you can get valuable feedback on your presentational skills from other people. In the following activity we suggest a systematic approach to gathering such feedback.

Activity: Making your presentations really successful

1. To make your presentations really successful try working through this section, gradually taking everything on board in your preparations.
2. When making presentations, ask your peers to give you feedback using the presentation feedback sheet that follows this activity.
3. After your presentation reflect on how you thought it went and on the feedback sheets you have collected from your peers. Key questions here are:

   - What went well?
   - What could be improved?
   - What would you do differently next time?

Presentation feedback sheet

	Excellent	Good	Acceptable	Needs attention!
1. Impact of the introduction				
2. Clarity of the message				
3. Structuring of the content				
4. Relationship with the audience				
5. Vocal projection (too loud / soft?)				
6. Effectiveness of body language				
7. Maintenance of eye contact				
8. Pace of delivery (too fast / slow?)				
9. Pitch of delivery (too high / low?)				
10. Management of time (on time?)				
11. Closure of session				
12. Overall quality of session				

Other comments:

When evaluating feedback, make a time to go over it and remember it does embody people's subjective opinions, so be prepared to ignore any one-off comments that don't make sense to you or fit in with the general view. For example somebody might criticise your time management when actually you finished right on time. Conversely if nineteen out of twenty people said you spoke too quietly, it is very likely that you did. It is not personal, you don't need to get upset, you didn't fail, you just need to speak louder next time.

In the end there is no substitute for experience in developing your presentational skills, so it is good to take every opportunity to practise and to develop your skills. Avoidance will only increase your level of anxiety, so don't avoid. Remember that you don't have to be perfect, but learning good skills, practising them regularly and learning from feedback will help you to improve and become a really effective presenter.

Follow-up activities

TIME FOR ACTION – CHECKLIST

Have you:

- recognised what stylistic conventions are important for writing up your work?
- thought about how to write developed introductions and summary conclusions?
- learnt how to structure your arguments in the main body of your report?
- recognised what you need to do to improve the graphic presentation of your work?
- appreciated the importance of avoiding plagiarism and of source referencing correctly?
- understood how you could improve your grades through feedback from tutor, peer and self assessment?
- considered what else you need to know in order to write an extended essay, thesis or dissertation?
- thought about what is required to give really effective presentations and to overcome any anxiety about speaking in public?

Further reading

Blumberg, B., Copper, D. and Schindler, P. (2005) *Business Research Methods.* Maidenhead: McGraw-Hill.

Boud, D. (1986) *Implementing Student Self-Assessment*. New South Wales: Higher Education Research and Development Society of Australia.

Burns, T. and Sinfield, S. (2008) *Essential Study Skills: The Complete Guide to Success at University*, 2nd edition. London: Sage.

Cameron, S. (2008) *The Business Student's Handbook*, 4th edition. Harlow: Pearson.

Churchill, H. and Sanders, T. (2007) *Getting Your PhD: A Practical Insiders Guide*. London: Sage Publications.

Cottrell, S. (2005) *Critical Thinking Skills: Developing Effective Analysis and Argument*. Basingstoke: Palgrave Macmillan.

Cottrell, S. (2008) *The Study Skills Handbook*, 3rd edition. Basingstoke: Palgrave Macmillan.

Feldman, R. (2000) *POWER Learning, Strategies for Success in College and Life*. Maidenhead: McGraw-Hill Higher Education.

Lee-Davies, L. (2007) *Developing Work and Study Skills*. London: Thomson.

Mounsey, C. (2002) *Essays and Dissertations*. Oxford: Oxford University Press.

Ridley, D. (2008) *The Literature Review: A Step-by-Step Guide for Students*. London: Sage.

Russell, T. (1994) *Effective Feedback Skills*. London: Kogan Page.

Saunders, M., Thornhill, A. and Lewis, P. (2006) *Research Methods for Business Students*, 4th edition. Harlow: Financial Times/Prentice Hall.

Seeley, J. (2002) *Report Writing*. Oxford: Oxford University Press.

Topping, K. J., Smith, E. F., Swanson, I., Elliot, A. (2000) 'Formative Peer Assessment Between Postgraduate Students', *Assessment and Evaluation in Higher Education*, Vol. 24, No. 2.

Walliman, N. (2004) *The Undergraduate Dissertation: The Essential Guide for Success*. London: Sage.

Websites to look up

- For further help with writing up reports and essays:

http://www.english.bham.ac.uk/staff/tom/teaching/howto/essay.htm
http://www.mdx.ac.uk/WWW/STUDY/gloess.htm

- For further help with source referencing and bibliographies:

http://www.ldu.leeds.ac.uk/plagiarism/how.php
http://www.uwe.ac.uk/library/resources/general/info_study_skills/harvelec.htm

Time for review and reflection

This is your space to log your reflections on this chapter, to think about what you have learnt, how you will use it and what else you need to find out.

What were the key learning points of this chapter?
What are your strengths in the areas covered by this chapter?
What areas did you identify for development?
What have you learnt about yourself?
How will you use it?
What else do you need to learn or find out about in relation to this chapter?

<table>
<tr><td>

8</td><td>

How to Develop Successful Examination Techniques</td></tr>
</table>

Overview – what's in this chapter?

- Why do you need to upgrade your examination skills?
- Why do many people fear examinations and why do some people fail?
- Planning for success, including positive thinking and visualisation
- Organising your revision systematically
- Preparing yourself for examinations
- What to do in the examination hall
- What to do afterwards
- Follow-up activities, further reading and websites to look up
- Time for review and reflection

Why do you need to upgrade your examination skills?

Try completing this short self-scoring test, to assess your own level of confidence in relation to improving your examination skills.

Activity: Why do you need to read this chapter?	
You need to self score each question on a scale from 0 to 10, where 0 is low and 10 is high.	
1. How confident are you about taking examinations?	
2. How organised are you in terms of your revision?	

3. How good are you at managing your time in the revision period?	
4. How effective have your revision techniques proved to be in the past?	
5. How easy do you find it to visualise your own success in exams?	
6. How well do you pick the right question in the exam hall?	
7. How good are you at organising your thoughts into answers in the examination hall?	
8. How competent are you at developing your answers in the exam?	
9. How good are you at managing your time in the exam hall?	
10. How confident are you about getting the grades you want?	
Total score	

Interpretation

What did you score?

- Less than 50%   You will definitely find a lot of help in this chapter.
- 50%–75%   There is still plenty to learn in this chapter.
- 75%–100%   You are very confident – read on to confirm your understanding.

Many people find examinations difficult and some underachieve. However, we believe that examination candidates can improve their performance by developing a range of appropriate techniques. These include not only systematic revision methods but also working on mental attitudes beforehand.

In this chapter therefore we first pose the question: 'Why do many people fear examinations and why do some people fail?'. We then turn to look at planning for success, including positive thinking and visualisation, organising your revision systematically, preparing yourself for examinations, what to do in the examination hall and what to do afterwards. Finally there are some follow-on activities, some suggested further reading, websites to look up, and some space for review and reflection.

Why do many people fear examinations and why do some people fail?

Virtually all examination candidates admit to suffering from a certain level of anxiety and this is hardly surprising – sitting at a desk in a large room in complete silence is not, for most of us, a daily activity. Some candidates do too much work and suffer from **burn out**, while many arrive ill prepared and some do not arrive at all.

Activity: Why do people fear examinations?

Try to answer the following questions:

- Why do you think that other people fear taking examinations?

- How many of these fears do you share?

Let us be clear, hardly anybody actually likes examinations, but to progress successfully through your course you will need to pass your exams. You don't want to become one of those students who has to take re-sits or repeat modules instead of progressing to the next year – or even to leave the course.

To succeed in examinations we suggest that you start from the position that you have the capability of passing, but doing this will require you to do three things:

- You will need to develop a positive psychological orientation, which we call **can do thinking**.

- You will need to have sufficient knowledge of your field of study and that will require systematic revision of course content.

- You need to develop your study skills in order to facilitate the first two points.

Developing your study skills will make the whole process a lot easier and less painful, because you will be more prepared psychologically, more efficient and thorough in your examination revision, and more effective in the examination hall. Therefore, we strongly recommend that you use the methods discussed in this chapter to develop your study skills and to support your preparation for all your exams.

Activity: Why do some students underachieve in examinations?

1. Review the following list of potential answers to the above question:

   - Inadequate preparation.
   - Being overcome by anxiety either beforehand and/or in the exam hall.
   - Not being able to recall what they want to say.
   - Answering the wrong questions.
   - Not reading the questions properly.
   - Answering the question they wished had been asked.
   - Poor time management/spending too long on one or two questions to the exclusion of others.
   - Writing too little and/or leaving early, feeling that you have done enough.

2. Have any of these been a problem to you? If so, this chapter should help.

Planning for success, including positive thinking and visualisation

We are all to some extent conditioned by our past experiences, for good or ill, so it is good to start your preparation by thinking about what happened before.

Activity: How are you with examinations?

Recall your previous experience of examinations and then answer the following three questions:

1. What went well?

2. What went badly or could have gone better?

3. What do you think you need to do differently next time?

What happened in the past does not necessarily determine the future. We can build upon the positives and overcome the negatives. In order to develop a positive approach to examinations we suggest that you consider taking the following steps:

- **Recognising anxiety is normal** – we need to recognise that a certain level of anxiety is quite normal in unfamiliar situations, but also that this anxiety can be controlled and it does not have to detract from our performance. See also Chapter 4 on handling stress and developing relaxation techniques.

- **Recognising your own motivation to succeed** – it is vitally important in the run up to examinations to remember why you are doing this course and to remember what your motivation is to succeed. We suggest that you review Chapter 1, Recognising your motivation to learn, grow and develop. Recognising your motivation can really help you to overcome your anxieties.

- **Eliminating the 'can't do' psychology** – we must avoid saying anything negative such as 'I just can't do exams' because this establishes and reinforces a failure psychology. You may find that some of your peers start the 'can't do' chat in the run up to examinations, focusing on how difficult it will be. It is good either to challenge this, if you can, or avoid it as much as possible if you can't.

- **Developing a 'can do' psychology** – we must look positively at examinations, developing a view which recognises that success is mostly dependent upon our having mastered a set of techniques which work for us, which we can learn and develop, and is focused upon what needs to be done to ensure success. We need to reflect this in what we do and say. It's not just a case of talking 'can do' but backing this up with actually doing what needs to be done. If you don't, then it is just arrogance, and that won't ensure you pass!

- **Visualising your success** – as well as talking, thinking, and acting positively, we can also practise a technique of positive visualisation. To do this we try mentally to picture ourselves revising systematically and then being relaxed and confident in an examination hall. Visualisation works by helping us to create some positive mental structures of an event before it happens, and thus we are more familiar with the situation when it arrives. See also Chapter 2, Visualising your success, on Neuro-Linguistic Programming.

- **Learning to relax** – finding ways to relax and unwind during the examination period will be especially important. Maintaining normal social contact and exercise can be good. Eastern techniques such as meditation, yoga or tai chi are also beneficial and may be worthwhile learning, not just for examinations, but to help us deal with all other stressful situations in life. See also Chapter 4, Handling stress and developing relaxation techniques.

- **Dealing with severe anxiety problems and phobias** – in cases of severe anxiety or actual exam phobia, it may be appropriate to learn a **relaxation response technique** together with **progressive desensitisation**. This involves learning a relaxation method while gradually being exposed to a perceived threat. Taking mock examinations, working through past papers, and visiting the exam hall may all offer opportunities for desensitisation. See also Chapter 4 on handling stress.

> **Activity: What do you need to do to approach your examinations more positively?**
>
> Review the list of bullet points in this section and consider what you will do differently in order to approach your examinations more positively.

Organising your revision systematically

While many students spend a great deal of time revising, not all their valuable time is well directed. In order for you to revise really well we recommend that you consider the following systematic approach.

- **Know what you are going to be asked to do**. Attend any revision lectures or seminars that are available and take careful note of what your lecturers are saying. Ask questions if anything is unclear and, if you can't do this, send your lecturer an email or try calling in to see him or her.

- **Inspect past papers**. These will indicate the style of question which has been asked in the past, but do not assume that this will remain the same. Examiners change from time to time, and so does the syllabus and subject area as both modules and whole academic disciplines evolve.

- **Make a realistic revision schedule**. Once you have worked out what is expected of you and what you need to do to succeed, it's time to organise your revision by making a daily schedule. Make sure your plan is realistic in terms of what you can achieve in the time. You won't necessarily stick to your schedule exactly, but you will need to be firm with yourself, so that if you get behind one day, you ensure that you do more the next to catch up.

- **Start revision early**. It is good to start as early as possible, firstly so you can use your valuable time productively. The old adage holds 'revision starts in September', the point being that you don't have to wait until teaching ends to start revising. Secondly, early revision is good because we learn best in bit-size chunks – little by little, bit by bit. It takes us time to really absorb material and to get a firm grip on it rather than a superficial understanding.

- **Recognise attention spans**. We all have a natural attention span after which we tend to switch off and become less productive. Because we learn best in short bursts, it is good to break big blocks of time into many short periods of intense study. For example a morning of study can be broken into several shorter periods. You can give yourself a little reward at the end of each period to help your motivation. See also Chapter 4 and its section on managing your time.

- **Review all your notes and handouts**. Re-read all material, making sure that you have a complete set of notes and that they are in a logical sequence. This will help you to remember the scope of the course you have taken, and thus make you aware of what might come up in the examination.

- **Reduce each topic to a series of key words or mind maps**. Remember that for the purpose of recall, your brain works much like a filing cabinet. By identifying key words you are attaching a **tag** and, from this, a whole file can potentially be recalled in the examination hall. Refer back to Chapter 5 on mind mapping.

- **Memorise the key words or mind maps**. Try writing them out several times if necessary, to build confidence in your ability to recall them. Take them with you to look at on the bus or train, put them up over your desk, bed or in the bathroom. The more times you look at them, the more it will help you recall them later on.

- **Use tricks to help you to remember**. You can use acronyms, word association techniques, colour coding, diagrams, cartoons, music or whatever else you find useful. These tricks will help you remember what you want and also to overcome the fear of drying up in the examination.

A student told us...

One student reported that she played a different piece of music when revising each topic. In the examination hall she sang the appropriate tune to herself and then was able to recall the particular content that was associated with it. This is an association technique in action.

- **Test yourself**. Try to write up model answers to previous exam questions. At first you will probably need to refer to your mind maps or key words, but later you can start an answer by copying them out from memory. Try to keep to the timescale you will have in the exam hall, so that you will know how much you will be able to write on the day. You may even attempt a full mock exam. All this helps to desensitise you to the exam experience and to build confidence. As with everything, we tend to learn by repetition.

- **Set up a study circle**. If you can recruit a reliable group of your peers, it can be useful to meet up every so often to review your progress, discuss topics and perhaps to give each other feedback on model answers. However, it's not good to rely on a study circle to do your revision for you. In the end you have to learn the required material yourself.

- **Don't do too much!** A very few students burn out by doing too much, so make sure you take regular breaks when revising. Try to give attention to normal activities such as eating, sleeping, diet, exercise and having social contact. See also Chapter 4.

A student told us ...

A final year student told us that she had worked night and day and tried to read everything in her discipline in the expectation of getting a first class honours degree. In the exam hall she felt totally confused and couldn't make sense of all the material. She came out with lower second and was very disappointed.

- **Don't do too little!** Far more students either fail or underachieve through the lack of systematic revision than burn out by overdoing it. We don't want you to be one of them, so it is a question of getting the balance right – and that comes back to having a workable revision schedule and making sure you activate it.

- **Avoid all last minute revision and mugging up**. Anything you do learn at the last minute is likely to confuse you. You will tend to focus on what you read last when constructing your answers, rather than giving a balanced account.

Activity: Organising your revision

- Review the bullet points in the previous section, making a note of all the ones you feel you need to pick up on.
- Find out exactly what will be expected of you in your examinations and what you will need to do to succeed.
- Make a realistic revision schedule for the period you have to revise, making sure you build in time for yourself.
- Turn your plans into actions and monitor your progress on a daily basis. Ticking off what you have done is a simple but effective way of both monitoring and recognising your achievement.

Preparing yourself for examinations

Once you have prepared yourself mentally for your exam and have your revision organised, it is also important to think about the practicalities. Check all your examination arrangements and make sure of everything beforehand. In particular you should check out:

- **Dates and times**. This might seem obvious, but check and re-check the dates and times of your examinations. It is not unknown for exam candidates to turn up at the wrong time and even on the wrong day.

- **Examination hall**. Do you know where the exam is being held? It may be in another building to the one where you normally study or even on a different campus. If it is not a familiar room to you it might be useful to go and have a look beforehand in order to avoid any last minute panic on the day. Also this helps to build familiarity and to desensitise you.

A student told us...

A former student told us that as an undergraduate, she ended up getting married inbetween the Milton to the Romantics and Shakespeare examination papers. They went on honeymoon for the three days between the two exams, where they took in a couple of plays. Upon their return, she sat the exam and got a first, but says now, 'I wouldn't advise it'.

- **Travel and parking etc**. It is also good to check your travel arrangements. If travelling by bus or train it may be safer to aim for the one before the one that would get you there on time, to give yourself some time in hand. If you are driving you will need to check out the parking arrangements and any restrictions. However you travel, be aware that if you have an early exam you may be caught in the morning rush – and you will need to allow for this too.

- **What you need to take with you**. What you need to take will vary considerably according to the discipline, but clearly pens will be required by virtually everyone plus pencils, rulers, etc. for many subjects. If it is an open book examination, be clear as to what you can take in. Does this include your file of notes? Can you take a dictionary into the exam?

- **The goodies you are allowed**. It is now common for students to take drinks, particularly water into exams. You may also be able to take sweets, chewing gum and perhaps a banana which can be useful for slow energy release. However, most institutions will draw the line at a packed lunch or a takeaway!

> **Activity: Preparing for your exam**
>
> 1. Review the bullet point list in this section, making note of all the ones you feel you need to pick up on.
> 2. Make sure you check out everything before the day of your examination.

What to do in the examination hall

Assuming that you have done all your revision and preparation, it is still important to think about what happens on the day, in the examination hall. It's a question of translating all your hard work into the results that you deserve. It is rather like being an Olympic athlete: you have done all the training and now you want that gold medal. Here are some things to bear in mind:

- **Check that all is in order**. You don't want a wobbly table or to be sitting in a draft. Do not be frightened to draw any problems to the attention of the invigilators, either before the exam commences or during it, by raising your hand. You deserve and should have a fair chance to complete your examination under acceptable conditions.

A student told us...

During the course of an exam a student told us that she was being distracted by the smell of an over-ripe banana. We found that the student behind her had the offending item of fruit on her table and we managed to negotiate its immediate disposal.

- **Complete your documentation**. As soon as you are allowed, complete the documentation required by your institution before your examination takes place. This will normally be on the front cover of your answer book and perhaps an attendance slip or other document. You will probably need your student number which you should take with you. If you forget it, raise your hand and an invigilator may be able to get it for you.

- **Read the paper carefully**. When you are allowed to, read all the questions and all the instructions very closely. Be sure to select the questions which will give you the best chance to show your ability. While it is useful to look for **content words** in questions in order to help you identify the topic, it is also important to recognise **action words** which tell you what the questions are asking you to do. For example, 'compare and contrast' is not the same as 'analyse'. See also Chapter 5, the section on understanding assessment, and in particular the distinction between action words and content words in assessment questions.

- **Know exactly what you have to do and do it!** Make sure that you know exactly what you are being asked to do. There are no extra marks for answering too many questions. You will lose marks by answering too few questions or indeed the wrong number from the various sections. So just do as you are asked!

- **Write essay plans**. Take a few minutes to write an essay plan for each question which you have selected, using your mental lists of key words or mind maps. You may find that you know more than you think. Do not be afraid to use knowledge gained from other parts of your course, particularly if you can show how topics link and connect.

- **Answer the question on the paper**. You should not simply regurgitate the essay which you have planned, but rather you should marshal the evidence and arguments which you have recalled in support of the answer which is required.

- **Write a suitable introduction**. Make sure that your introduction tells the examiner that you have understood the question. If it is appropriate, define terms or concepts mentioned in the question. You can also describe how you will be answering the question. What you say here will signal to the examiner that you are a competent student, capable of answering the question.

- **Make points into paragraphs**. You can answer questions by writing paragraphs around points which you have listed or key words from your mind map.

- **Write suitable conclusions**. Make sure that your conclusion pulls everything together by summarising your arguments and makes it clear that you have understood and answered the question. Remember, do not introduce new material at this stage.

- **Write clearly and use space**. Try to write clearly so that your examiner can read your work and use space to present your work as clearly as possible. Start a new page for each answer and make it clear which question you are answering. Your examiner may have to read hundreds of exam scripts, so be kind to him or her.

- **Use all your time productively**. Make sure that you spend an equal amount of time on each question, assuming that they command equal marks. By all means avoid giving more time to your favourite topic or concentrating on earlier questions at the expense of later ones.

A student told us...

A student told us that upon reading his exam paper, he was pleased to see a question on the very subject of his recently completed dissertation. He started writing all he knew on the subject and completely lost track of time. When he completed the answer he realised that two and half of the three hours allowed had elapsed, but that he had only written one of the three required essays. He then quickly wrote up a couple of note form answers. Although he did pass the exam, it was with a grade far below his expectations.

- **Don't re-read or check over the paper unless you have spare time**. Many tutors will tell you to re-read or check over your paper before handing it in, but this may not be the most productive thing to do. If you still have things to say or work to do it may be better to keep working until the invigilators call time. The argument is that you will probably score more marks from the extra work than you would have lost by correcting the odd point here and there.

> ### Activity: Making your time in the exam hall really count
>
> - Review all the bullet points in this section and make a note of what you think you need to do in the exam hall.
> - If you have found exams difficult in the past, think carefully about what you need to do differently next time.

What to do afterwards

Some students become unduly worried by what happened in the examination hall. It can be really useful to have a 'post mortem' with your peers in order to chat over how it went. However, the important thing to recognise is that there is nothing more you can do; you can't change a thing and it is now time for you to relax until you get the results.

Your tutors will not want to talk to you about your examination performance while they are marking and when examination boards are still in progress. Your work will normally be marked anonymously and your grade recorded by your student or examination number, so they won't know your grade at the marking stage nor will they be allowed to discuss it with you.

When you get your results you will hopefully be pleased. If you are disappointed it may be worth contacting your tutors. Even if they cannot talk specifically about your performance, you may be able to talk over with them how you think the exam went. If you have to re-take, it will clearly be important to understand where you may have gone wrong and you might get some pointers for the future.

Follow-up activities

> **TIME FOR ACTION – CHECKLIST**
>
> Have you:
>
> - checked out what you need to do to achieve the results that you want?
> - made a realistic revision schedule and built in rewards for yourself?
> - reviewed all your notes and handouts?
> - made mind maps or other study aids?
> - reviewed previous examination papers and given yourself mock attempts?
> - checked out the venues, times and dates of your exam; made sure that you can find the venue and arrive in good time; and know what you need to take with you?
> - done your best in the examination hall, selected the right questions and used all the time productively?
> - remembered to relax afterwards?

Further reading

Burns, T. and Sinfield, S. (2008) *Essential Study Skills: The Complete Guide to Success at University*, 2nd edition. London: Sage.

Cameron, S. (2008) *The Business Student's Handbook*, 4th edition. Harlow: Pearson.

Cottrell, S. (2006) *The Exam Skills Handbook*. Basingstoke: Palgrave Macmillan Ltd.

Cottrell, S. (2008) *The Study Skills Handbook, 3rd edition*. Basingstoke: Palgrave Macmillan.

Feldman, R. (2000) *POWER Learning*. Maidenhead: McGraw-Hill Higher Education.

Websites to look up

- For help and support in preparing for and taking examinations:

http://www.student-counselling.ed.ac.uk/selfhelp/ExamSuccess.htm
http://www.jcu.edu.au/student/assessment/examinationsuccess/index.htm

 # Time for review and reflection

This is your space to log your reflections on this chapter, to think about what you have learnt, how you will use it and what else you need to find out.

What were the key learning points of this chapter?
What are your strengths in the areas covered by this chapter?
What areas did you identify for development?
What have you learnt about yourself?
How will you use it?
What else do you need to learn or find out about in relation to this chapter?

PART 3 HOW TO DEVELOP JOB/WORK PLACEMENT SEARCH AND CAREER BUILDING SKILLS

<table>
<tr><td>

9

</td><td>

How to Understand the Job, Internship or Placement Search Process and What is Required for Success

</td></tr>
</table>

Overview – what's in this chapter?

- Why do you need to upgrade your skills in order to find a job, internship or placement?
- Why there are winners and losers in the job, internship or placement search process.
- Finding a job, internship or placement
- Matching your skill set to the job, internship or placement you apply for
- Follow-up activities, further reading and websites to look up
- Time for review and reflection

Why do you need to upgrade your skills in order to find a job, internship or placement?

Try completing this short self-scoring test, to assess your own level of confidence in relation to the search for jobs and placements.

Activity: Why do you need to read this chapter?	
You need to self score each question on a scale from 0 to 10, where 0 is low and 10 is high.	
1. How clear are you about what sort of job, internship or placement you will want to do?	
2. How confident are you in searching for jobs and placements?	
3. How aware are you of where to look for jobs or placements in your chosen field?	
4. How much do you know about graduate employment websites?	

(Continued)

(Continued)

5. How much do you know about the 'milk round'/employment fairs?	
6. How aware are you of what employers will be looking for from you?	
7. How good are you at identifying your own unique skill set?	
8. How good are you at analysing what job advertisements are really looking for?	
9. How good are you at matching your skill set to jobs or placements?	
10. How confident are you in your ability to get the kind of jobs and placements you want?	
Total score	

Interpretation

What did you score?

- Less than 50%   You will definitely find a lot of help in this chapter.
- 50%–75%   There is still plenty to learn in this chapter.
- 75%–100%   You are very confident – read on to confirm your understanding.

There are winners and losers in the job search process, so it is important to make sure that you get the best job you can and this means taking the sort of steps outlined in Chapters 9, 10 and 11. The steps outlined include:

- Correctly identifying your skill set and how it might be developed.

- Matching your skill set to job, internship or placement vacancies offered by potential employers.

- Presenting yourself in the best possible light at every stage in the process.

Feeling confident that you will have good skills to offer to a potential employer – whether for part-time employment to help with living expenses while you are studying, for an internship or placement, upon graduation, or for making progress in your career – can contribute to your motivation to do the necessary hard work to obtain good marks in all your assessments.

Placements form an essential component of some courses and if you have the option to take one we strongly recommend it. In our experience most placement students have a really valuable time out, doing real jobs and applying theory to practice in the workplace. **Internships** tend to be shorter and often occur over the summer vacation, but still offer the opportunity of some real work experience. Short periods of **work shadowing** can also provide an opportunity to observe somebody else who is doing a real job and offer you valuable insight.

We have often been asked why we include job search material in our year one undergraduate skills programme and it is suggested that this is really a final year concern. However, we see that early consideration of your job search options allows you to plan your path ahead, to review progress towards your goals at regular intervals and to change them if necessary. Your planning can also inform your choices of elective modules, placements or internships and the subject of dissertations.

Job search skills are not just for graduate employment, as if this were not important enough in itself. These skills can be practised and honed while you are in higher education, first in helping to obtain the part-time, weekend and summer employment which is often so vital in supporting your finances, secondly for gaining suitable placements and internships which are frequently very competitive, thirdly for graduate employment, and finally within your professional careers, where they may be used to facilitate both changes of employment and internal promotion.

In our experience, final year undergraduates are already busy making applications and frequently attending assessment centres as well as dealing with all the pressure of completing final year assignments and examinations. Therefore, final year is too late. The idea of developing job search skills as an end of course activity misses the point and the opportunity for planning, preparation and rehearsal throughout your course.

In this chapter we will first look at how you might become a winner rather than a loser in the job search process, at the skill set you have and how this might be matched to job vacancies, and then at where you might find and how you might search for jobs, internships and placements. Finally there are some follow-on activities, suggested further reading, websites to look up, and some space for review and reflection.

Why there are winners and losers in the job, internship or placement search process

Although most graduates get jobs, not all students are successful in the job search process, not all get the jobs they want and not all are well matched to the job they get.

There are two parties to the recruitment and selection process. The employer should logically be trying to employ the best person for the job. Their task is to describe jobs accurately and then to organise the recruitment and selection process in order to deliver the best people they can find to do the job concerned. Similarly, you might logically want to find the job to which are best suited and, if so, your task is to describe and present yourself both accurately and positively in order to secure such a position.

While selection decisions are ultimately down to employers, success in the job search process is partially within your control and this has implications for every stage in the process. In particular this will involve you in understanding:

- Who you are, what you have to offer and how you can match this to job vacancies, and internship and placement opportunities.

- How to describe and present yourself in written documents – such as application forms, curriculum vitae and cover letters – in order to make a positive impact upon the reader and to influence their decision to invite you to an interview or assessment centre.

- How to present yourself at an interview or at an assessment centre and what you can learn from unsuccessful applications (see Chapter 11 and the section on appointment or rejection and how to handle it).

It might be useful to regard the whole recruitment and selection process as a giant matching activity in which candidates are matched with jobs. Your responsibility as the applicant is therefore to go through the job search process in such a way as to present yourself as clearly and accurately as possible in order to find a successful match. It is similarly incumbent upon employers to describe jobs, internships and placements accurately.

Activity: What are employers looking for?

- Imagine you are the administrator dealing with recruitment and selection in the human resource or personnel management department office of a large employer. You have 500 application forms or curriculum vitae on your desk and your task is to produce a shortlist of twenty candidates for interview or assessment centre.
- What would you be looking for in the documentation in order to pick the best people to invite? Try making a list of things that you would see as essential and desirable.
- When you have worked your way through Chapters 9, 10 and 11 review your list. How does what you have learnt affect how you would present yourself to employers?

Finding a job, internship or placement

Your chances of finding the job, placement or internship which is best suited to your skills and talents will be significantly enhanced by casting your net as widely as possible. As suggested earlier, you are strongly advised to make a shortlist of possible jobs rather than relying on just one that you have set your heart on. In order to give yourself the best chance in the job search process we suggest that you consider looking at the following sources of information:

- **Internet sources** – today Internet searches in one sense make the job search task a lot easier, although in another sense you may have more to choose from and it may prove quite time consuming. Internet sites fall into two basic types:

  - **Recruitment sites** which offer jobs from a wide range of employers and within a range of specialisms. Several are aimed directly at graduate employment such as Prospects, Graduate Monster, etc. (for a selection of URLs see the Websites to look up section of this chapter).

  - **Employer sites** which will often have a recruitment or vacancies link (for a selection of URLs see the Websites section of this chapter). If you have an idea about a company you might like to work for it's always worth making a search to see what they are offering. If you don't see anything, try making contact directly. They may be able to direct you to another source or put your details on file.

- **Newspapers** – tend to have different types of jobs on different days or in particular supplements such as 'education', 'public appointments' and 'scientific', etc. These often provide a useful snapshot of the employment situation within a particular sector of the labour market in terms of the jobs and salaries on offer.

- **Specific trade magazines and journals** – provide an invaluable source for jobs in sometimes highly specialised fields of employment. Again they provide a useful snapshot of a distinct sector of the labour market.

- **Recruitment agencies/recruitment consultants** – are common in certain industries not only for recruiting 'temps' but for many other positions. Head hunting agencies specialise in recruiting people from other companies for particular jobs.

- **University careers office and departments** – will hold a lot of information but also should have a certain level of expertise in dealing with people from your course and in your specialism. You will probably be able to see a careers counsellor who can give you further help and guidance.

In addition to exploring all of the recognised sources there is also merit in talking to your tutors, who will often have links with employers, and to your peers who will be going through the same sort of searches as you. Sharing ideas with your peers can save time and positions which they reject might be perfect for you. However, you may also find yourself in competition with them for the same jobs.

Activity: Finding positions to apply for

- Investigate all the sources listed earlier in this section.
- Identify a number of possible vacancies that could be the focus of your search.
- Think carefully about each vacancy. Ask yourself: Is this one I might reasonably expect to get? Is that one I might actually be interested in applying for in the future? Be prepared to focus your effort on a number of promising vacancies.
- Approach the organisation for application/employment information.
- See also Chapters 10 and 11 for help in completing the application requirements and selection procedures successfully.

Matching your skill set to the job, internship or placement you apply for

Understanding what you have to offer

The first stage in your job search process lies in understanding what you have to offer to employers and, in particular, what is special about you. This can then be matched against the requirements of specific jobs that you have identified.

There are many ways of identifying what you have to offer. A good starting point might be to think about your course – what aspects do you particularly like, what might you want to develop in your career? Internships and placements are an opportunity to put 'a toe in the water' before you commit yourself to a long-term career.

Throughout this book we have asked you to consider aspects of yourself, your skills and what you need to develop – particularly in the final sections of each chapter where we have invited you to review and reflect upon what you have learnt. Taking some time to review what you have written would also be a useful step in understanding what you have to offer employers.

In particular, it would be useful either to complete a new **personal SWOT analysis** or to update the one you made previously, outlining your perceived strengths, weaknesses or areas for development and barriers you might face (refer back to Chapter 2 and the section on completing a personal SWOT analysis).

The next activity will help you identify your skill set, but the list is not exhaustive and you might want to add other skills that you have – especially ones which are particular to your discipline. We find students often forget very important skills for which they do not hold an academic qualification, such as speaking more than one language, being able to use various computer packages, together with other qualifications such as holding a driving licence, first aid certificate or sports coaching badge.

Activity: What skills do I have to offer?

Complete the Personal Skills Inventory below, by rating yourself out of 10 in the following categories (0 is low and 10 is high).

People		Activities	
Ability to get on with people from different backgrounds		Creativity, design and layout	
Ability to see and understand other people's points of view		Lateral thinking/thinking 'out of the box'	
Dealing with the general public		Ability to see the 'whole picture'	
Teamwork		Being good at argument and debate	
Managing other people		Making decisions	
Teaching or training others		Managing change and transition	
Negotiating		Setting priorities	
Helping others to arrive at decisions		Working out agendas	
Being sensitive to others' feelings		Organising work to meet deadlines	
Caring for others		Staying calm in a crisis	
Ability to read other people's body language		Problem solving	
Dealing with others by phone		Reading complex texts	
Ability to cope with 'difficult' people		Word-processing	
Speaking clearly and to the point		Computer literacy	
Being able to take direction from others		Working with numbers	
Courage to speak out against injustice		Analysing information/data	

(Continued)

(Continued)

Determination and perseverance		Classifying and organising information (e.g. filing)	
Ability to set own goals		Facilitating meetings	
Maintaining a high level of motivation		Selling	
Ability to take responsibility for own actions		Interviewing	
Trust in my abilities		Listening and hearing	
Personal qualities		Asking questions	
Ability to recognise own needs and ask for help		Handling practical things	
Ability to learn from mistakes		Seeing how things work	
Stress management		Writing formal reports	
Willingness to take risks and experiment		Writing official letters	
Assertiveness		Form filling	

- Review the above scores.

- What did you learn from this exercise?

Understanding what the employer is looking for

A good employer will take time to conduct a thorough job analysis in order to know what they are looking for. Traditionally this was usually done by means of writing a job description which described the role and a person specification which described the person who might be expected to fill it. While some employers may still take this approach, the person specification is now seen to have potentially adverse implications for ensuring equality of opportunities and encouraging diversity among employees (Cornelius, 2001: 39–40). Therefore, many employers are now describing jobs in terms of **job competencies**, which are seen to avoid some of the potential problems of person specification.

Job competencies have been defined as:

> one of the sets of behaviours that the person must display in order to perform the tasks and functions of a job with competence. Each competency is a discrete dimension of behaviour. (Woodruffe, 2000)

At root, a competency is something that someone could do, such as 'can work as part of a team' or 'can demonstrate analytical ability'. A competence can potentially be tested at various stages in the recruitment and selection process and in particular at assessment centres (see Chapter 11 on assessment centres).

Before advertising an internship, placement or job, an employer will normally analyse the role and decide the key competencies required. In an internal review of skill competencies mentioned by employers in 86 placement job descriptions/job details, being offered to students at Brighton Business School in 2006, we found that the following three competency areas stood out:

- **Basic information technology** – 80 per cent mentioned this including competency in using 'Word', 'Excel', email and sometimes 'PowerPoint'.

- **Verbal communication skills** – 74 per cent mentioned this and in particular the ability to communicate at all levels in the organisation and with customers.

- **Team working skills** – 63 per cent mentioned this requirement.

What becomes clear, both from this survey and from casual observation of job advertisements, is that there are a relatively small number of core competencies which many employers are looking for and that mastery of these will be very important both in gaining internships and placements, and in achieving successful graduate employment and careers.

Matching your skill set and aspirations with employer expectations

Once you have a clear idea of what you have to offer and what employers are looking for, it's time to try and match the two together. Your search should be as wide as is practical in order to try and identify your best chance of getting into something that you really want to do (see the following section on finding a job placement or internship).

If you are going to make an application that will have a good chance of success it is important to have as much information as possible about the job and the organisation. If you have a job advertisement this is really a starting point and will give you only limited information. Some ideas for expanding your knowledge include the following:

- Look at the company website. They will probably have a recruitment or vacancies link and you may find much more information there – perhaps a job description or list of competencies.

- Contact the organisation and ask if there is a recruitment pack which they can send you. This will be quite normal for internship, placement, graduate entry level and higher positions.

- Ring the person dealing with the recruitment and selection for the position concerned to see if you can have a chat about what is involved. They may be very helpful, but avoid pressing them if they are not, as they might remember you as the awkward one on the phone!

If you are unable to get clear details of a job, it can also be useful to try to think yourself what might be involved and what might be required of you in terms of the competencies of the job concerned. Looking at similar jobs with other employers can sometimes throw some light upon what might be required.

It is good to aim high but applying for jobs which you have no realistic chance of getting or are ill matched for will not only waste your time, but also that of the employer. It is also good to make your own shortlist of the most suitable jobs for you and to pursue several applications at the same time. The one you set your heart on may not come up but another certainly will, if you are well organised and persistent.

Activity: Matching jobs to your unique skills set

- Select and review details of a job, placement, or internship you think you might be interested in.
- Are any job competencies listed? If not, identify what you think the employer might be looking for in a competent employee.
- How do these competencies match up against your skill set?
- Consider also which things would be hardest to demonstrate if you applied.

Follow-up activities

TIME FOR ACTION – CHECKLIST

Have you:

- considered why you might need to upgrade skills in order to obtain a suitable job, internship or placement?
- explored a range of sources and identified a number of suitable positions to apply for?

- recognised what employers are looking for in the job/internship/placement search process?
- reviewed what you have to offer to employers?
- matched your skill set to the job, internship or placement you are applying for?

Further reading

Byham, C. and Cox, J. (1988) *Zapp! The Lightning of Empowerment: How to Improve Productivity, Quality and Employee Satisfaction*. New York: Random House.

Cameron, S. (2008) *The Business Student's Handbook*, 4th edition. Harlow: Pearson.

Guirdham, M. (2002) *Interpersonal Skills at Work*, 3rd edition. Harlow: Pearson.

Herbert, I. and Rothwell, A. (2005) *Managing Your Placement: A Skills Based Approach*. Basingstoke: Palgrave.

Woodruffe, C. (2000) *Development and Assessment Centres*, 3rd edition. London: CIPD.

Websites to look up

- For further information on careers and development:

http://www.nusonline.co.uk/info/careers/

- Some graduate job search sites to explore:

http://www.get.hobsons.co.uk/index.jsp
http://www.Milkround.com
http://graduate.monster.co.uk/
http://www.prospects.ac.uk
http://www.targetjobs.co.uk/graduate-jobs/

- Some leading companies which have graduate entry programmes include:

http://www.asdagraduates.com/
http://www.ibm.com/employment/uk/graduates/
http://www.kpmgcareers.co.uk/Home_(1).aspx?
http://www.unilever.com/ourcompany/careers/workingwithus/default.asp
http://www.hewlettpackard.com
http://www.pwc.com/uk/eng/careers/main/index.html

Time for review and reflection

This is your space to log your reflections on this chapter, to think about what you have learnt, how you will use it and what else you need to find out.

What were the key learning points of this chapter?

What are your strengths in the areas covered by this chapter?

What areas did you identify for development?

What have you learnt about yourself?

How will you use it?

What else do you need to learn or find out about in relation to this chapter?

<table>
<tr><td>

10

</td><td>

How to Understand the Application Process in Order to Get Shortlisted

</td></tr>
</table>

Overview – what's in this chapter?

- Why do you need to upgrade your application skills?
- Developing content for the application process that will attract a potential employer
- Completing application forms to present yourself in the best light
- Developing your CV in order to gain maximum impact
- Writing cover letters that employers will want to read
- What to do if you don't get shortlisted for interview or assessment centre
- Follow-up activities, further reading and websites to look up
- Time for review and reflection

Why do you need to upgrade your application skills?

Try completing this short self-scoring test, to assess your own level of confidence in applying for jobs and placements.

Activity: Why do you need to read this chapter?

You need to self score each question on a scale from 0 to 10, where 0 is low and 10 is high.

1. How successful have you been in making applications in the past?	
2. How accurate are you in describing yourself in the application process?	
3. How well compiled and presented is your curriculum vitae?	

(Continued)

(Continued)

4. How good are you at completing a convincing application form?	
5. How competent are you at writing effective cover letters?	
6. How good are you at the graphic presentation of documents?	
7. How good are you at proof-reading your own work?	
8. How open are you to receiving feedback on your job search documents from a valued reader?	
9. How open are you to receiving feedback from employers on any unsuccessful applications?	
10. How confident are you in your ability to get the kind of jobs, internships or placements you want?	
Total score	

Interpretation

What did you score?

- Less than 50%   You will definitely find a lot of help in this chapter.
- 50%–75%   There is still plenty to learn in this chapter.
- 75%–100%   You are very confident – read on to confirm your understanding.

You may feel that you don't need to give attention to this chapter because you have achieved success in job applications in the past or perhaps you just consider it to be form filling. However, when you apply for higher level jobs, the bar will be higher and so you will need to raise your game in order to succeed. Many decisions between applicants are close, with many having similar qualifications, so making sure you get the edge over someone else may come down to how well you describe your skills and qualities and express yourself.

What you are doing is selling yourself in the labour market and, therefore, your application documents are effectively your advertising material. If someone gave you a tatty and uninformative leaflet advertising a company, you would no doubt be unimpressed. The analogy is clear; you have one chance to impress the employer and to get shortlisted for interview or assessment centre, so it is very important to present yourself in the best possible light.

In this chapter we look at what you can do to improve your application documents including application forms, curriculum vitae (CV) and cover letters. We also touch on what to do if you should make an unsuccessful application. Finally there are some follow-on activities, some suggested further reading, websites to look up, and some space for review and reflection.

Developing content for the application process that will attract a potential employer

What you say about yourself will be very important in matching your skills and talent to the job concerned. Work done here identifying content can be used not only in your job search documents – such as your curriculum vitae, application and cover letter – but also in what you say at an interview or assessment centre.

In Chapter 9 (Matching your skill set to the job) you identified your key skills and these should definitely be part of what you say about yourself during the application process. However, your personal qualities are also part of what makes you special and in the following activity we ask you to identify them.

Activity: What are my personal qualities?

1. Try to pick your top 10 personal qualities from the list below and then place them in order of preference.

     1. ....
     2. ....
     3. ....
     4. ....
     5. ....
     6. ....
     7. ....
     8. ....
     9. ....
    10. ....

flexible		loyal		consistent		thoughtful
articulate		responsible		team player		cautious
calm		dedicated		innovative		imaginative
organised		versatile		committed		patient
punctual		creative		careful		dependable
tactful		good under pressure		strong		dynamic

(Continued)

(Continued)

sensible alert quick reliable practical cooperative polite ability to work alone		approachable hard working assertive capable accurate thorough perceptive		competent direct humorous adaptable decisive enthusiastic bright		friendly methodical outgoing self motivated serious sensitive trustworthy likeable	

2. If you already have a CV on file, you might want to review it to see if your personal qualities are emphasised in it. If not, what are you saying about yourself?

Using active verbs

As well as describing your skills and qualities accurately in the job search process, it is also important to think about how you express yourself. Using active verbs in your job search documents and when you are talking about yourself at an interview or during an assessment centre, will help you to project an image of an active, doing person. Some examples of active verbs include:

coordinating	**leading**	**handling**	**writing**
growing	**travelling**	**managing**	**planning**
caring	**developing**	**communicating**	**supervising**
advising	**diagnosing**	**training**	**driving**
persuading	**filing**	**researching**	**translating**
recruiting	**assessing**	**selling**	**selecting**
establishing	**sorting**	**teaching**	**enabling**
performing	**analysing**	**deciding**	**reading**
serving	**negotiating**	**compiling**	**drawing**

Using the STAR technique to get your message across

When describing the competencies employers require, it is very easy to ramble and not use the best example or include enough detail/information in the answer.

The STAR technique (Byham and Cox, 1988) provides a framework to construct a relevant answer to open-ended questions asked during an interview or when completing an application form. The STAR technique enables you to structure what you have to say as follows:

- **S = Situation** – outlines a situation that demonstrates that you possess a personal quality or skill.

- **T = Task** – describes a task which you have completed.

- **A = Action** – explains what you actually did in this situation.

- **R = Result** – reports the result of your actions.

A STAR is really a little story, which you are proud of and which can be told to your advantage. The STAR technique gives you a format in which to tell stories about yourself. Some examples of the type of STARs which people construct include:

- You were the captain of a successful sports team or a key member of a team which succeeded in its endeavours.

- There was a crisis and you saved the day, as in someone drowning or needing the kiss of life.

- You were at work and there was a crisis which you managed to resolve.

- You found something personally very hard but overcame this in order to succeed.

- You achieved a personal goal. Perhaps you climbed a mountain, made a speech, acted in a play, played in a band, and so on.

- Through sheer hard work you got a place at university.

Many questions found in application forms and indeed asked at interviews are actually quite predictable, as for example:

- What are your strengths?

- What are your weaknesses?

- What do you think you could bring to the job/company?

You can prepare STARs which describe your strengths, but also rehearse ones to cover your weaknesses. One way of handling questions about weaknesses is to describe an area in which you were once weak but, through perseverance and hard work, have turned into a strength. For example you might have found the quantitative aspects of your course very hard or were extremely nervous about making oral presentations. If you worked on a weakness and it then became a strength, you will have demonstrated some admirable qualities to the employer. If you are aware that you currently have weaknesses, try to describe these as 'areas to develop', perhaps making clear that this is the next step in your personal development.

Activity: Making a STAR

Try making a STAR for one or more of your top 10 personal qualities and another to cover an area of weakness.

- Situation or task

- Action

- Result

Completing application forms to present yourself in the best light

Planning your application form

Visual presentation will be the first thing which the reader sees, so your application must look good, but content, grammar, syntax and spelling are also very important. Try taking the following **systematic approach**:

- Follow the instructions – for example, write in black ink.

- Analyse the job advertisement and any other information you have been sent about the company or job, doing further research and telephoning the company if this is appropriate. Refer back to Chapter 9 and the section on matching your skill set to the job, focusing on understanding what the employer is looking for.

- Organise your content before you start writing, giving accurate information about your-self that is tailored to the job concerned, i.e. avoid *nice to know* in favour of *need to know*. Use the **STAR** technique to complete questions asking for examples (see section above).

- Demonstrate your ability to present yourself positively, avoiding negative statements and making sure that you stress your **personal qualities**. See also the previous section of this chapter.

- Use **active verbs** in order to stress your positive abilities as a capable *doing* person (see also the section above).

- Photocopy your application form and complete a draft before you commence writing up the final version. This allows you to make all the mistakes on the draft rather than the final copy.

- Make sure your handwriting is consistent in style, size and justification.

- Check your spelling and then get someone else to read your first draft if possible, as it is easy to miss your own mistakes.

- Photocopy the completed application form so that you can re-read it before interview, also, you may be able to use it as the basis for another application form.

Activity: Completing an application form

- Try completing a draft application form for a job, placement or internship you are interested in, using the systematic approach described in this section.
- Get a valued reader to proof-read your application form, as it is easy to read over and miss your own errors. It is also a good way to get positive feedback and con-structive criticism. Be prepared to accept constructive criticism, but remember that at end of the day it is your application form and should say what you want to say about yourself.
- Finally, write up your completed application form and post it or submit it online.

Developing your CV in order to gain maximum impact

What should my CV contain?

The content of a CV or curriculum vitae will vary from individual to individual and, while there are many suggested formats, you have to consider what is appropriate to our own situation and the positions you are applying for. We do not believe in providing a model CV which you might copy, but rather we want to make suggestions which might usefully inform your own design.

The following list provides an idea of the content of a typical CV:

- **Personal details**, including: name, address, telephone number, mobile number, fax number, email address (to make yourself easily contactable), nationality and date of birth.

- A brief **personal profile** of yourself.

- **Education** including schools, colleges, universities attended, together with dates and qualifications obtained.

- **Professional qualifications** held.

- **Any other qualifications** you hold (e.g. first aid certificate, driving licence or sports coaching badge).

- Details of your **current or last job** and previous **employment history**, including: dates, job title, responsibilities, employer's name(s) and any 'in-service' training.

- **Personal interests** and any other **personal skills or talents** you think you have.

- **Referees** – give names, titles, addresses, telephone numbers and email/fax if available/applicable.

Activity: Deciding on content for your CV

- Review the typical CV content listed in this section and then brainstorm what particular content you will want to put in your own CV.
- What would be suitable sub-headings to use?
- When you have decided upon content, think about what sequence it should go in.
- When you have decided upon what you want to say about yourself, try to put your ideas under headings that are relevant to you and your life and experiences.

What is a personal profile?

A personal profile is a short description of yourself which helps the reader to come quickly to a view as to whether you might be suitable for the job. It is rather like visiting a book shop and just reading that small panel on the back of a book that describes the content. Though it may not instantly make up your mind to buy the book, it can prompt you to read further and look longer at the book, rather than returning it swiftly to the shelf.

Sadly, those who have the task of reading a great many CVs will not stop to read all that is submitted thoroughly, so the inclusion of a personal profile can help them match the right person with the right job more easily and including such a short synopsis might just give you the edge.

Activity: Completing a personal profile

- Draft a personal profile of 30–40 words (maximum).Try to include what is relevant to say about you.
- Now show your draft to a valued reader in order to get feedback.

CV construction

There is no 'correct' way to structure the material in your CV, but some formats may prove more effective than others in getting you a job. It is good to change the format of your CV when applying for different types of jobs, giving greater or lesser emphasis to various sections of your content, as appropriate to the job concerned.

Don't try to say everything you possibly could, because your CV will be too long and the reader will lose interest. Similarly, don't 'sell yourself short' by saying too little. Try to keep a balance. The 'normal' length of a CV in Britain is two sides whereas in some countries it is only one. However, for a senior post it might be much longer, where age is expected to have brought more experience which needs to be reported.

There is no need to put the words 'curriculum vitae' or CV at the top of the first page, because inevitably you will be sending it with a cover letter starting with something like 'Please find attached my curriculum vitae'. We don't head up letters with the word 'letter', so why do it to a CV? Instead, why not put your name in large print, to help reinforce your name and really sell yourself.

Try to think about the initial impact your CV will make. There is a sense in which the visual aspects of your CV may actually be more important than the content, simply because it is the first thing they will see. It is very important therefore to consider how it looks and to give attention to layout, spacing, indents, justification, fonts, etc. The more professional your CV looks, the more likely it is that the reader will take your application seriously and want to read the content.

The first page of many CVs is extremely boring, often containing only bare details such as name, contact information and qualifications, with nothing which is particularly influential in terms of getting a job. Including your personal profile after the name and contact details can help greatly, as will saying something more about your experience of education rather than just listing schools, colleges and qualifications.

When listing jobs, courses attended or qualifications and so on it may be more useful to put the most recent information first. For example the placement or internship you did last year might be much more interesting and important than the holiday job you did three years ago. Similarly your university level qualifications will be much more important than those you achieved at school.

Make sure you include all the personal qualities which you think are important and use active verbs (see the earlier section of this chapter on developing content for the application process).

Finally include the names and contact details of referees that you can rely upon at the end. You should include at least two referees; one should be an academic reference and another can be a current or past employer, if you have one. In general, try to avoid personal references. Some people put 'references supplied on application', which is simply a pointless irritation to a potential employer. Why not just put them in?

Activity: Completing your CV

- When you have completed the previous two activities, try to write up a draft CV, giving attention not only to the content but also to the layout.
- Next look at your CV from a distance, far enough away so that you can't read the actual words. How does it look? Try to visualise yourself as a potential employer, and consider what impression it gives and whether you would be encouraged to read the content.
- Get someone else to proof-read your CV, as it is easy to 'read over' or miss your own errors. This is also a good way to get positive feedback and constructive criticism. Be prepared to accept constructive criticism, but remember that at end of the day it is your CV, and should say what you want to say about yourself.
- Finally, write up your completed CV.

Writing cover letters that employers will want to read

Your cover letter is another opportunity to sell yourself in the application process and, as with your CV and application form, how it looks may be as important as what you say. In writing cover letters we suggest that you follow the following conventions:

- Always use an acceptable and up-to-date business format for a cover letter.

- Address the letter correctly, quoting any name, department, etc.

- Quote any reference numbers that are given.

- Include a title or heading in bold, stating the position applied for and where it was sourced, after the salutation (e.g. Dear Mr Jones) and before your opening paragraph.

- State the purpose of the letter in the opening paragraph.

- Try to start the letter with something more creative than 'I am writing...'.

- Include only relevant details in the letter, rather than repeating items from the CV and application form.

- Where the salutation was **Dear Sir or Madam** close with **Yours faithfully**. Where it was addressed to a named individual such as **Dear Ms Smith**, close with **Yours sincerely**.

- Print and sign your name.

Activity: Writing effective cover letters

1. Review the following letter in the light of the previous list of points to see how many errors you can find.

Flat 4,
147 Hanover Street
Brighton,
East Sussex,
BN2 4XX

11 July 2008

Miss S Wiseman,
Graduate Recruitment Officer,
Norwich Union
PO Box 4
Surrey Street
Norwich
NR1 3NG

Dear Stephanie Wiseman

Graduate Marketing Programme

Norwich Union is one of the 15 largest companies in the UK with a cliental of approximately 15 million people world wide. I am very interested in finding out more about the graduate marketing scheme that that you have available.

(Continued)

(Continued)

As an applicant who has a great understanding of the importance of branding and customer relations I believe that my skills and enthusiasm would be an asset to your company. I have a proven track record in the field of customer care in retail and service sector. I enjoy a challenge and as a graduate with a business and marketing degree I believe that I successfully meet your requirements.

Please find enclose my curriculum vitae, and above my contact details I am available for interview at any time.

Yours faithfully,

2. What did you learn from reviewing this letter which might inform your own construction of cover letters?

3. Try drafting your own cover letter and then get some feedback on it from a valued reader.

What to do if you don't get shortlisted for interview or assessment centre

If a job application is unsuccessful, don't be afraid to ask for feedback on your application as many employers are now very willing to give it. What you learn can be used to revise your job search documentation and, potentially, can help you to get the job, placement or internship you want next time. See also Chapter 11 and the section discussing appointment or rejection and how to handle it.

Follow-up activities

TIME FOR ACTION – CHECKLIST

Have you:

*   considered why you need to upgrade your application skills?
*   developed content for the application process that will attract a potential employer?

- recognised what is required in order to complete application forms that will present you in the best light?
- developed your CV in order to gain maximum impact?
- understood how to write cover letters that employers will want to read?
- thought about what to do if you don't get shortlisted for interview or assessment centre?

Further reading

Byham, C. and Cox, J. (1988) *Zapp! The Lightening of Empowerment. How to improve Productivity, Quality and Employee Satisfaction.* New York: Random House.

Cameron, S. (2008) *The Business Student's Handbook*, 4th edition. Harlow: Pearson, Chapter 17.

Guirdham, M. (2002) *Interpersonal Skills at Work*, 3rd edition. Harlow: Pearson.

Herbert, I. and Rothwell, A. (2005) *Managing Your Placement: A Skills Based Approach.* Basingstoke: Palgrave.

Lee-Davies, L. (2007) *Developing Work and Study Skills.* London: Thomson.

Woodruffe, C. (2000) *Development and Assessment Centres*, 3rd edition. London: CIPD.

Websites to look up

- Information on careers and development:

http://www.nusonline.co.uk/info/careers/

- For further help with CVs, cover letters and application forms:

http://www.get.hobsons.co.uk/advice/job-applications
http://www.prospects.ac.uk/cms/ShowPage/Home_page/Applications_CVs_and_
  interviews/p!eefmd
http://www.grb.uk.com/making_applications0.0.html
http://www.e4s.co.uk/graduate-jobs/free-application-form-tips.htm

 # Time for review and reflection

This is your space to log your reflections on this chapter, to think about what you have learnt, how you will use it and what else you need to find out.

What were the key learning points of this chapter?

What are your strengths in the areas covered by this chapter?

What areas did you identify for development?

What have you learnt about yourself?

How will you use it?

What else do you need to learn or find out about in relation to this chapter?

11 How to Give Yourself the Best Chance of Success in the Selection Process

Overview – what's in this chapter?

- Why do you need to upgrade your skills for the selection process?
- Preparing for interview, including research and personal presentation
- Planning for success, including positive thinking and visualisation
- Developing your interview skills
- Performing effectively at assessment centre
- Appointment or rejection and how to handle it
- Follow-up activities, further reading and websites to look up
- Time for review and reflection

Why do you need to upgrade your skills for the selection process?

Try completing this short self-scoring test, to assess your own level of confidence in relation to the selection process for jobs and placements.

Activity: Why do you need to read this chapter?	
You need to self score each question on a scale from 0 to 10, where 0 is low and 10 is high.	
1. How successful have you been in the past at interviews or assessment centres?	
2. How good are you at preparing for interview?	
3. How important do you consider researching the employer to be?	

(Continued)

(Continued)

4. How important do you consider analysing the job to be?	
5. How good are you at formulating questions to ask at interview?	
6. How good are you at being interviewed?	
7. How are your teamwork and leadership skills?	
8. How good are you at completing problem-solving activities?	
9. How likely are you to ask for feedback if you are unsuccessful?	
10. How confident are you in your ability to get the job, internship or placement you want?	
Total score	

Interpretation

What did you score?

- Less than 50%   You will definitely find a lot of help in this chapter.
- 50%–75%   There is still plenty to learn in this chapter.
- 75%–100%   You are very confident – read on to confirm your understanding.

Developing a clear understanding of the recruitment and selection processes, being well prepared and presenting yourself in a good light at interview or assessment centre, will all help you to secure the position you want.

It is important to realise from the outset that, when you submit your application, you are entering a competitive situation. This will perhaps become most obvious when you arrive to find a number of other people waiting for interview or when you are part of a group invited to an assessment centre. When you talk to the others you may find that they have similar backgrounds and qualifications to yourself, and then it may become really obvious that how good your preparation has been and how you perform on the day will tend to determine if you are successful or not.

The main purposes of this chapter are to help you prepare for interviews and to appreciate the special considerations for achieving success at assessment centres. As with many other things in life, good preparation will help you to achieve a good result. In particular you should consider what research you need to do, your analysis of the job, together with how you present yourself on the day.

The chapter will also look at how to handle success. What to do if you don't get the job – to help you handle rejection – is also discussed and includes getting feedback and learning from the experience. Finally there are some follow-on activities, some suggested further reading, websites to look up, and some space for review and reflection.

Preparing for interview, including research and personal presentation

Researching the organisation

It is important to make sure that you know as much as possible about the organisation and their business. Your research can include internal sources such as the information which they sent in an application pack, the company website and annual report. However, you should also aim to find independent sources including newspaper and journal articles, in order to see what other people are saying about the organisation. It may also be interesting to see what the organisation's competitors are saying or doing and to look at the market in which they operate – to see what is happening and what is on the horizon.

Try to find out what is really happening with the organisation concerned rather than just relying on the organisation's own propaganda. Most employers will appreciate the time you have taken to find out about their business and will ask you if you want to ask them any questions. This is your chance to show that you know what you are talking about. They will expect you to have questions for them, so make sure that you have some prepared! See also the section below, Developing your interview skills, especially the part on formulating your own questions.

Analysing the job

A good employer will have broken down the job using a system of job analysis and perhaps created job competencies (see Chapter 9 on matching your skill set to the job, especially the part on understanding what the employer is looking for). You may have been sent a job description or list of job competencies as part of an application pack. In this case it is worth taking some time to match this to your skill set and to ask yourself where your strengths and weaknesses are. You can then be prepared to stress your strengths in relation to the job concerned and also ready to cover any weaknesses. See also Chapter 10 on developing content for the application process and the discussion in this chapter on answering the question.

If no information is provided on the position concerned, it is very useful to do your own job analysis before the interview or assessment, in order to anticipate the type of questions you might be asked. If the job is particularly specialised or unusual, it may be appropriate to ring up beforehand and to try and get more information on what is required.

Personal presentation

Employers will not only judge you on what you say but also on how you look – and this includes physical appearance and body language. Appearance may well be as important as what is said, in respect of who gets a job. We strongly suggest you take note of the following in particular:

- **Think about how you dress**. Formality is the norm in most professions, so a smart and business-like appearance will be expected by most employers and they will appreciate the effort you have taken. Even where the normal dress code is more relaxed, try to be as smart as possible for interview.

- **Do not let minor details let you down**. For example dirty fingernails or chipped nail varnish may appear distasteful to your assessor or interviewer. If you have to eat on the way to the interview, take some chewing gum to clean your teeth and freshen your breath.

- **Be aware of your body language**. If you slump in the chair, you will appear sloppy to your interviewer. Crossed arms and legs can be a sign of defence and will give the impression that you are hiding something. Fidgeting and restlessness will make you look nervous (see also Chapter 3 on recognising non-verbal communication).

- **Remember to maintain appropriate eye contact**. If you don't look your interviewer in the eye when answering a question, you will look dishonest and will be unlikely to secure a position. If you are facing an interview panel, it is best to look mostly at the person whose question you are answering, but also look at the other panel members from time to time to keep them interested in you and what you are saying.

In general, you should try to present yourself in the best light. Everyone else will probably be doing so, so why not give yourself the best chance of getting the job?

> ### Activity: Preparing for interview or assessment centre
>
> - Take a few minutes to review this section and then make a checklist of everything you need to do before your next interview or assessment centre.
> - After an interview or assessment centre, take a few minutes to review how it went and to think how your preparation could be improved another time.

Planning for success, including positive thinking and visualisation

Arriving for an interview in the right frame of mind is clearly important but frequently overlooked. Developing a positive mental attitude can really help you achieve a good result at interview or assessment centre, but it doesn't happen automatically. There are a number things which you can do to get in the right state of mind to be more successful at interview and these include:

- **Good preparation** – as discussed earlier in this chapter. Doing thorough research and preparation will make you feel more confident, because you will have more to talk about in the interview and you will also be ready with your own questions.

- **Positive thinking** – this involves spending time thinking positively about the job and visualising yourself doing it. You can also imagine yourself at the interview being positive and relaxed. Doing this will create positive connections in the brain, rather than the negative ones which build up when we are apprehensive. Try thinking **can do** rather than **can't do**. See also the section in Chapter 2 on visualising your success.

- **Stress control and relaxation techniques** – giving attention to this area will mean that you will not arrive at the interview or assessment centre 'shaking like a jelly'. Learning to breathe and meditate will help you to stay focused in the interview and can be usefully combined with visualisation techniques. If necessary, you can learn a **relaxation response technique**. See also Chapter 4 and the section on handling stress and developing relaxation techniques.

- **Planning your journey** – this may sound obvious, but arriving late can be a wretched experience: it will give a bad impression and can definitely undermine your confidence, at least to start with. It is important to check whatever instructions you were sent, to print off maps and/or routes and study them, and to check train times. A good rule when taking trains is to take the train before the one which would get you there just in time.

- **Use your time before the interview or assessment centre productively** – once you have arrived, take some time to prepare yourself and focus your thoughts.

> ## Activity: Developing a positive mental attitude
>
> - Take a few minutes to review this section.
> - Make an action plan of what you need to do in order to develop a positive mental attitude towards interview or assessment centre.

Developing your interview skills

At interview you have only a short time to impress the employer, so developing good interpersonal skills that are appropriate to the interview situation is essential. Key areas for consideration are developing your listening skills, answering questions effectively and formulating your own questions to ask.

Developing **active listening skills** involves learning to listen more and say less. The first step in answering questions successfully is to listen to what was asked. This may sound absolutely obvious but under the pressure of the interview it is all too easy to miss the point or to jump to conclusions. Listening is an important skill which can be developed with a little work. See Chapter 3 on questioning and active listening skills.

Learning to answer the question that was asked and not being evasive may be crucial to your success. This includes being honest and saying if you don't know the answer if that is the case. Many interview questions are, however, quite predictable. The most commonly asked questions at interview tend to revolve around asking you what your strengths and weaknesses are, although they may be disguised in various forms such as:

> **'What do you think you could bring the company?'**

> **'What areas do you see as being most important to your future development?'**

While it is important to answer the question that you were asked, it is also really useful to have developed some stock responses that can be adapted to the question. This preparation can help you avoid drying up and can give you more things to talk about. One way of structuring your answers is to use the STAR technique (refer back to the section in Chapter 10 on developing content for the application process). A STAR is essentially a little story you tell about yourself and, in this context, STARs typically fall into two categories:

- **Achievements** – things you are proud of and want to relate. These can really help highlight your strengths.

- **Problems you have overcome**. These can help you express weaknesses in the context of how you overcame them. You thus turn a weakness into strength and so provide a positive way of answering a negative question.

Two students told us...

Two of our students told us the following stories as a result of preparing STARS:

'I was captain of football at school when we got to the final of the local cup competition. We were one goal down with ten minutes to go, but I managed to reorganise things and gee everybody up. We scored a couple of quick goals to win the cup 2–1'.

'I found that I was rubbish at maths when I got to university, but I went to the library and got more books to work through. I also saw my tutor and she went over some stuff with me. I talked to the best student in the group and she did the same for me. In the end I passed all the quantitative tests OK and now I feel more confident about doing it'.

As part of your preparation for an interview it is useful to have prepared a number of 'STARS' which you can pull out in response to appropriate questions. In a Chapter 10 activity we invited you to make a couple of STARS and also suggested how you might deal with questions about your weaknesses. In the following activity we invite you to prepare a couple more, but five or six might be a more realistic total to have prepared before attending an interview or assessment centre.

Activity: Developing answers to standard interview questions

Try to develop answers to the following common interview questions, using the STAR technique:

1. What are your strengths/what might you bring to the job?

   - Situation or Task

   - Action

   - Result

(Continued)

(Continued)

---

2. What are your weaknesses/what areas do you need to develop?

- Situation or Task

- Action

- Result

Your answers at interview should always be consistent with what you said in your application documents. Not telling a consistent story would be viewed with great suspicion by any prospective employer. The easiest story for you to tell will be the honest one and we strongly recommend that you don't act and that you don't lie at interview or assessment centre. You are not trying to win an Oscar and it will surely show through at interview or assessment centre if you are trying to act a part. It is **you** that needs to shine through at interview. Similarly, lying will tend to show up and look very bad. No one wants a dishonest or untrustworthy employee on their payroll.

A manager told us...

A manager told us that if he suspected that an interview candidate was lying, he would ask more and more questions on the subject he was suspicious about. As he got into more depth he would tend to expose a liar because they either could not answer the question or would tend to make up more or more ridiculous answers.

Prospective employers will normally expect you to ask them questions at some stage in an interview and having some intelligent questions to ask will be essential if you are to make a good impression. This may also require you to improve your own question formulation skills by asking more *open ended questions* in order to get them talking to you. See also Chapter 3 for discussion of questioning and on developing your interview skills.

You will need to have a good range of questions prepared as some of what you expect to ask many have been covered in the interview. It is not unusual for interviewers to start by giving you a short briefing, perhaps covering the organisation and the position concerned.

Interviewees' questions tend to fall into a range of categories, including:

- The organisation and its business.

- What the job involves.

- Opportunities for your future development within the organisation, including professional qualifications, training, development and career path.

- Where you are likely to be located and what scope there is for mobility in the future.

- Terms and conditions of employment if these are unclear or if the salary is negotiable.

- It might not be a good idea to start by asking questions about your own needs. The overriding concern of your interviewers is much more likely to be what you might do for the organisation rather than the reverse, so this list might usefully be seen as an order of priority for your interview questions.

Activity: Developing questions for your interview or assessment centre

- Before attending interview or assessment centre, prepare a list of questions that you might want to ask and put these into a priority order.
- After an interview or assessment centre, take a few minutes to review how it went. How useful or relevant were your questions and what could be improved another time?

Performing effectively at assessment centre

What are assessment centres and why do they need special attention?

An assessment centre can be defined as a selection procedure using multiple methods. Such centres tend to be used by larger corporations for recruitment to graduate/management training schemes, student placements and are also sometimes used to monitor progress and for promotion decisions. The time and cost involved tends to deter the use of assessment centres for other positions.

An assessment centre might typically last a full day and perhaps longer. During this time the employer will use a variety of methods to test a range of competencies which have been identified as being appropriate for the job concerned (see also Chapter 9 and the section on matching your skill set to the job, focusing on understanding what the employer is looking for).

Whereas a traditional interview effectively tests only a limited range of competencies such as knowledge and interpersonal skills, an assessment centre test can test a variety of competencies and so the organisation can develop a more thorough appraisal of the individual applicant. There is, therefore, much less chance that anyone can 'talk their way into a job' without having the competencies needed for success in the role.

To succeed at assessment centres requires some special considerations, but the skills which you are likely to be called upon to demonstrate are for the most part the ones we have been looking at in this book and which you will have been developing both through your course and your life experiences.

Each activity you complete at an assessment centre will be scored, most probably against a range of competencies, so it may be a mistake to try and think, 'what are they looking for in this one' and then try and perform in a different way for that task. The scores will probably be weighted and then aggregated at the end of the assessment centre to produce a points total for each participant, from which the actual selection decisions will be made.

Many people find the experience of attending assessment centre surprisingly enjoyable, especially so the team and social aspects. Perhaps the most important thing to remember is that you are attending something serious, which requires your full attention and considerable energy if you are to come out well.

A consultant told us…

A consultant who has specialised in setting up assessment centres for major businesses comes to talk to our students every year. He told us that when he was attending assessment centres in his final year as an undergraduate, he had been given no preparation and found the experience very difficult.

What activities might an assessment centre comprise?

The range of assessment centre activities which you might be called upon to participate in are many and various, but they are likely to include:

- **Psychological tests** – these will tend to be either cognitive which relates to testing mental states or perhaps psychomotor which test mind–body coordination.

- **Practical aptitude test/work simulation** – this will involve either doing practical tasks similar to the work concerned or real tasks which are part of the work role being tested for.

- **Role plays and re-enactments** – role plays will ask you to play a role in a fictional interpersonal situation, such as dealing with a problem customer. Re-enactments are similar but based upon real situations. In either case you may find yourself facing a professional actor, who will really test you.

- **Individual problem-solving activities** – these will test your ability to work alone. Frequently this involves an 'in-box' or 'in-tray' exercise in which you are asked to read a number of documents within a limited time period and to sort them into priority order for action or perhaps to suggest what action would be appropriate.

- **Group/team problem-solving activities** – these will test not only your ability to solve problems but also your skill competencies in working with others in a team. Perhaps your leadership skills within the team may also be tested.

- **Interview** – just because you are at an assessment centre, it doesn't mean that you won't have an interview. In fact it is highly likely that you will. The interview element should therefore be taken seriously, as it might be the opportunity for you to sell yourself on an individual level.

- **Social activity** – be aware that you may be being assessed at any time – or indeed all the time – that you are at the assessment centre and, therefore, how you conduct yourself in breaks and at meal times may also be important. For example, if you take your food from the buffet and sit quietly in a corner, avoiding all social contact with other people, this might well be observed.

Activity: Preparing for assessment centre

- Take some time to think positively about a forthcoming assessment centre.
- Consider the types of activity that might be involved.
- What special considerations will you make in preparing for assessment centre?

Appointment or rejection and how to handle it

Dealing with selection decisions

Whether you attend an interview or assessment centre, you will clearly be getting some good or bad news as a result. If you are offered a position and you decide to accept it, then it is just a matter of tying up the details of when and where you start. Alternatively, if you get a rejection it can be a very negative emotional experience – and all the more so if you truly wanted the job concerned. However, rejection can also be a positive learning experience and an opportunity to upgrade your skills for the next occasion.

Selection decisions tend to produce some very strong emotional reactions, which is not surprising – after all, they may affect the rest of your life. Therefore the emotional side needs to be dealt with and the result put in perspective. The tendency is either to feel that you failed or that the employer may have got it wrong, but neither is a useful or productive way to think about the situation. When you get a rejection, there a number of points which may be useful to consider:

- Unlike an examination in which an infinite number of people can pass, the jobs on offer tend to be finite. For example, if one hundred people apply for a job, ten get shortlisted for interview and you come second, this is not failure. You may in fact have been more or less equal with someone else who got the position but the employer may have made a marginal decision, such as the other person being able to start earlier.

- Remember that recruitment and selection is essentially a matching process and you might genuinely not be the right person for the particular job concerned. You may need to apply for different jobs or to different organisations where you will more likely be seen as the right person for the job.

- Your details may be kept on file for future reference and you may be called back for another position. Many employers do this as it saves re-advertising, re-interviewing and most of the other selection costs.

- If an employer doesn't hire you try not to see it as a problem, because there are many others you can apply to and you will have a good chance of getting a suitable position with one of these. You only need one job and the right one might be the next one that comes up.

It is important to express how you feel, however, so you may want to talk to a trusted friend. They will doubtless have an opinion to offer, such as 'they must be mad not to take you' or 'you are too good for them anyway'. However supportive your friend is, in the end you have to come to your own view and writing the experience down, as in the next activity, can really help.

> ### Activity: Off-loading and reconceptualising the decision
>
> - Start by writing down exactly how you feel, no matter how bad it is or how negative you are feeling. It is good to express it all.
> - Try to write something positive about what you have learnt or gained from the experience.

How you get informed

There are a number of ways in which employers inform candidates, all have problems associated with the process and none are ideal. The options include:

- Asking everybody to stay until the end of the day, so that candidates can be offered the job in turn until somebody accepts. This does get things settled straight away but does, of necessity, mean that everybody has to stay until it is resolved and to make a decision without much opportunity to consult friends and family etc.

- Asking candidates to sit by the phone on the evening of the interviews, again so that the position can be offered to candidates in turn.

- In writing – this inevitably creates delay, as the position has to be offered to each person in turn as some may not reply quickly and may need to be chased up.

However, if you are applying for an internship, placement, or graduate/management training scheme rather than a specific position, the process may be somewhat easier. You may get an indication on the day, but most likely you will hear by post. If you are attending assessment centre, it will be very unlikely that you will hear anything on the day as assessors will tend to have a 'washing up' meeting after all the candidates have left, at which they will reflect on the performance of all individuals attending.

By the end of an interview or assessment centre, the employer should have told you how you will be informed of the outcome, but if not you will need to clarify this. When you are applying for a number of positions there can be real problems in juggling all the interviews and assessment centres. It may be that you get offered a job before you attend the interview or assessment centre for the job you really want. This is a real dilemma and you may have to consider accepting the first job while still participating in the selection process for the second.

Learning from the experience

If you are unsuccessful at interview or assessment centre, it is now quite normal to ask for some feedback from the organisation concerned. In many larger and more sophisticated organisations they will have information on file from which they can give you some feedback. Sometimes what you learn is that there was nothing wrong with you or the way you presented yourself, but rather that you were not seen as the best person for the particular job concerned.

If no feedback is available from the organisation, it will still be important for you to consider how it went: what went well and what you could improve upon another time. If you are applying for several jobs, internships or placements at the same time the important thing will be to learn from each situation. If you can do this and you can improve your performance with each interview or assessment centre, securing a position will become all the more likely.

> **Activity: Asking for feedback and upgrading your job search skills**
>
> - Ask the organisation concerned for feedback on your performance.
> - Make a list of your strengths in the process and a list of what you could have done better.
> - Consider what you might do differently another time.

Not getting a job, internship or placement can seem like a real disaster at the time but often, in hindsight, we can see that it made possible our getting something different, perhaps something better or something to which you were more suited. As stated earlier many decisions are marginal ones, so the most important things to do are: do not to take the decision personally but rather use the experience to learn, grow and move on.

Follow-up activities

> **TIME FOR ACTION – CHECKLIST**
>
> Have you:
>
> - considered what you need to do to upgrade your skills for interviews and assessment centres?
> - thought about what you need to prepare for interview, including research and personal presentation?
> - given attention to planning for success, including positive thinking and visualisation?
> - recognised the importance of developing your interview skills, including preparation of STARS and your own questions to ask?
> - understood what is required to perform effectively at assessment centre?
> - thought about appointment or rejection and how to handle it, including asking for feedback from employers who give you a rejection? Have you thought about what you learnt and how you might use it in the future?

Further reading

Byham, C. and Cox, J. (1988) *Zapp! The Lightning of Empowerment: How to Improve Productivity, Quality and Employee Satisfaction*. New York: Random House.

Cameron, S. (2008) *The Business Student's Handbook*, 4th edition. Harlow: Pearson.

Guirdham, M. (2002) *Interpersonal Skills at Work,* 3rd edition. Harlow: Pearson.

Herbert, I. and Rothwell, A. (2005) *Managing Your Placement: A Skills Based Approach.* Basingstoke: Palgrave.

Mehrabian, A. (1971) *Silent Messages*. Belmont, CA: Wadsworth.

Woodruffe, C. (2000) *Development and Assessment Centres*, 3rd edition. London: CIPD.

Websites to look up

- For information on careers and courses etc.

http://www.nusonline.co.uk/info/careers/

- For help with interview skills:

http://www.bemyinterviewer.co.uk/index.html?utm_source=Google&utm_medium=PSE&utm_term=interview+skills&utm_campaign=BMI
http://www.careers.brad.ac.uk/graduate/jobhunting/interview.php
http://www.e4s.co.uk/graduate-jobs/free-interview-tips.htm
http://www.graduate-jobs.com/gj/gco/Booklet/graduate-job-interview-technique.jsp
http://www.get.hobsons.co.uk/advice/interview-job

- For help with assessment centres:

http://www.get.hobsons.co.uk/advice/interview-selection-centre
http://www.graduate-jobs.com/gj/gco/Booklet/graduate-job-assessment-centre.jsp
http://www.kent.ac.uk/careers/selection.htm

 # Time for review and reflection

This is your space to log your reflections on this chapter, to think about what you have learnt, how you will use it and what else you need to find out.

What were the key learning points of this chapter?

What are your strengths in the areas covered by this chapter?
What areas did you identify for development?
What have you learnt about yourself?
How will you use it?
What else do you need to learn or find out about in relation to this chapter?

12 How to Continue Developing
Yourself for your Future Success

Overview – what's in this chapter?

- Why do you need to continue developing yourself and upgrading your skills?
- Developing yourself in higher levels of education
- Developing yourself within your professional career
- Dealing with work role transitions, unexpected changes of circumstances and drawing on your own transferable skills
- Self-employment and entrepreneurship as an alternative to employment
- Developing your commitment to lifelong learning, personal growth and development
- Follow-up activities, further reading and websites to look up
- Time for review and reflection

Why do you need to continue developing yourself and upgrading your skills?

Try completing this short self-scoring test, to assess your own level of confidence in relation to your continued personal and professional development.

Activity: Why do you need to read this chapter?

You need to self score each question on a scale from 0 to 10, where 0 is low and 10 is high.

1. How likely do you think it is that you will continue to develop yourself after higher education?	
2. How much do you know about the concept of continuing professional development?	

(Continued)

(Continued)

3. How confident are you about continuing your education by taking professional qualifications?	
4. How confident are you about continuing your education by taking higher level academic degrees, such as a masters or a doctorate?	
5. How confident are you about dealing with planned changes of work role?	
6. How confident are you about dealing with sudden and unexpected changes of work role or redundancy?	
7. How confident would you be about starting your own business?	
8. How confident would you be about self-employment?	
9. To what extent have you considered developing yourself outside of work and employment?	
10. How confident are you in planning your own future personal growth and development?	
Total score	

Interpretation

What did you score?

- Less than 50%   You will definitely find a lot of help in this chapter.
- 50%–75%   There is still plenty to learn in this chapter.
- 75%–100%   You are very confident – read on to confirm your understanding.

There will be a life after higher education and this will provide you with new possibilities for growth and development, together with opportunities to learn new skills to add to your skills set.

In this chapter we look at the opportunities afforded for your continued development both by a return to higher education and also in your professional career. In your future life there will be many transitions to negotiate in a rapidly changing world and you may even find yourself made redundant at some stage. The good news is that you now have a set of transferable skills which you can use to help you move on successfully, so that change situations can become further opportunities to grow and develop.

We also explore self-employment and entrepreneurship which are both valuable and preferable alternatives to employment for some people, for all or some of their working lives. Lastly we look at the concept of **lifelong learning**, which potentially goes far beyond both higher education and even the problem of earning a living. Finally there are some follow-on activities, some suggested further reading, websites to look up, and some space for review and reflection.

Developing yourself in higher levels of education

When you are immersed in your course it is all too easy to see the end of your course as the end of your time in education. When revising for final examinations or struggling to complete a dissertation by the deadline, you may think 'never again'. However, if you have learnt good skills as outlined in this book, you will no doubt find your next degree a lot easier than your last.

In taking a higher degree you will have to learn some new skills, but these can be seen as building upon what you did before. For example, if you wrote an under-graduate dissertation, a postgraduate thesis should not prove to be too difficult, though perhaps longer and more rigorous in terms of academic standards.

It is often good to take a break after one degree before the next, although some people like to keep going and sometimes fear stopping. Taking a break can allow you to establish yourself in your profession or career, but there is always the danger of not getting back into studying.

You may find that your employer will give you some study leave; some may pay your fees or at least make a contribution. This support is more likely to be given, the more closely the degree you take is linked to your work. Taking a vocationally orientated degree can improve your chances of both internal promotion or changing jobs altogether.

An ex-student told us...

One ex-student told us that he had taken a first degree in literature with our university when he was young. He had then drifted through a series of jobs in travel and the tourism industry before finally getting into health service management. After a few years he was able to take a part-time masters degree in this field with us, which has now helped him to secure a senior management position.

In taking higher degrees, such as a masters or doctorate, you will normally be expected to learn more independently and there will tend to be less contact time than at undergraduate level. At masters level you should look to see how much is comprised of taught components and how much is independent supervised study. In a **taught masters** there is normally an element of supervised dissertation work.

If you are taking a research degree such as **Master** or **Doctor of Philosophy**, the emphasis will be on you working autonomously. Students sometimes talk about the 'lonely road' and you will need a high level commitment to the project and considerable self motivation. The project will normally be expected to break new intellectual ground, be a significant re-working of existing evidence, or perhaps both.

Supervision will be a key factor in completing a research degree. Finding somebody who is going to be interested in your work and able to support you is so vitally important that it may influence your choice of institution more than other factors such as location and facilities, which you will be using much less than on taught programmes. Sometimes research students select a university which is quite far away from their home and work in order to get the right supervisor. Actual supervisions will be fairly infrequent, but you may need to use their facilities from time to time, so location does need some consideration.

Professional doctorates have developed in recent years, enabling practitioners in certain professions to base doctoral work on more practical work-based problems. They frequently involve attending workshops with other practitioners in the same field and writing up a series of papers rather than a single thesis.

Activity: Thinking about going back into higher education?

If you are considering a return to higher education it is well worth taking some time to click around websites to gather information on your options before talking to institutions directly. Here are some critical questions to ask yourself:

- Why do I want a higher degree?
- Do I have the time, commitment and motivation to complete it?
- What problems or barriers would I have to overcome to complete the course?
- At what level would I expect to re-enter education?
- What qualification would I be seeking?
- Where would I want to study and is there a specific institution or department or supervisor I would want to work with?
- How much is it going to cost and who is going to fund this?

Developing yourself within your professional career

In many work organisations, particularly the larger ones, there will be an established programme of **continuing professional development**, often known as **CPD**. This may well be closely linked to appraisal and employee development programmes. In these cases professional development planning may be seen as the norm for all staff. Alternatively it might be restricted to certain types or grades of staff and there may be a requirement to opt in.

A good question to ask an employer at initial interview or assessment centre, and perhaps upon promotion, is what provision will be made for your continuing professional development (see Chapter 11, Developing your interview skills, especially on question formulation).

If you have a choice of jobs, a major factor in your choice might well be the extent to which your continuing professional development is likely to be supported and the potential there is for your development within the organisation. While the starting salary and rewards package might seem the most obvious attraction, particularly after some years of financial struggle as an undergraduate student, having scope for development might outweigh this in the long term.

In most professions CPD is organised by the professional bodies but, where there is no organised programme of CPD or indeed no effective programme, you will have to take responsibility for planning your own continuing development. In this case some of the skills learnt in this book should stand you in good stead – in particular those discussed in Chapter 2 on how to plan your personal development.

Dealing with work role transitions, unexpected changes of circumstances and drawing on your own transferable skills

In life we must expect that things will not always go smoothly. The days of a 'job for life' are now largely gone, so we must all be prepared for change. This will almost inevitably mean a series of **work role transitions**. However, each transition can be seen as an opportunity to grow, develop and learn new skills. When we make these work role transitions we take with us many **transferable skills**. Skills learnt in one role will form a sound foundation for the next and can even form the basis of a new career. Each transition can, therefore, be seen as an opportunity for growth and development.

If you join a large employer there may be scope to move around within the organisation, and this can provide a valuable opportunity to learn and grow. Alternatively you may want to look outside the organisation in order to see what else is on offer. It is good to practise some lateral thinking every so often and to take stock of where you are and where you hope to get to. See also Chapter 2 on personal development planning.

There are often new opportunities and new directions we could take if only we took a little time to recognise them. **Inertia**, in terms of employment, is the tendency to stay stuck in the same role for no particularly good reason other than that it avoids changing. **Redundancy** is not uncommon and, while this can prove to be traumatic at the time, it can be seen as providing an opportunity to take stock and look at how you can take what you have learnt into a new role. Sometimes the new role will be less well rewarded, at least in the short term, but it may also open up new opportunities for growth and development.

There could be a danger towards the end of your career of becoming a **time server**, who is just 'treading water' until retirement. It seems sad that last phase of your employment should be the least fulfilling and therefore it is good if you can make a contribution until the last. One obvious area is in passing on your skills and developing those who come after you. Another may be to seek a **secondment** to another organisation, normally in the public or voluntary sector, where your skills can be utilised over a set time period.

Eventually, **retirement** will become another transition for most of us. In many cases this can be planned and prepared for well in advance. Many retired employees use their skills set to good effect, either in the voluntary sector or in part-time employment.

Self-employment and entrepreneurship as an alternative to employment

For much of the last part of this book we have focused upon gaining employment and developing a career. The assumption has been that you will be working for others. However, the skills that you develop in higher education and also perhaps in employment can be a basis from which you may move into self-employment and perhaps entrepreneurship – working alone or starting a business with others.

Moving out of formal employment is a bold step and not for the faint hearted, but the rewards can be great, not only in financial terms but also in respect of personal autonomy. To put it more simply, you become your own boss. However, it is important to realise that for every successful small business there are many failures. While this should not stop you, it is important to have a well worked out proposal.

If you need to raise **capital** from banks, other financial institutions or venture capitalists, they will expect a well-researched business plan covering all aspects of the business including marketing plans and financial projections. Some of the skills learnt in education and beyond should help you with this, but the banks themselves often provide useful literature and support, as do local small business and enterprise units.

If you have gained marketable skills in employment you may decide to become a **freelance professional**, perhaps doing much what you did before but for a number of organisations rather than just one. Consultancy and training are popular routes and allow people to draw upon old contacts as a starting point, indeed some people even find themselves doing work for their former employer. This can be attractive to both parties as the ex-employee provides both continuity and flexibility. However, the freelance professional has no guarantee of work and must quickly establish a reputation and an independent client base.

A further alternative is to become a **portfolio worker**, possibly mixing a variety of occupations, perhaps working for a number of employers and often working on a self-employed basis. It can be an interesting and varied life and the mix of work which you do can change over time. The downside can be when you are either in demand on all fronts and it becomes difficult to satisfy all the demands or when everything goes quiet at the same time.

Some ex-students told us...

Three graduates who had initially worked in the public sector and who are all now self-employed told us their stories. One is a gardener and homeopath, another is running her own employment agency, while the third is both a professional gliding instructor and a central heating engineer.

Developing your commitment to lifelong learning, personal growth and development

The end of your studies can be a difficult time, after the intensity of student life, and for most there will be the transition into paid employment. For the majority of graduates full-time employment will be the next big step in their life and, of course, they will want to establish themselves in their new job. **Lifelong learning** might seem at this point as a rather abstract notion. However, we want to suggest to you that your long-term success and happiness will very likely depend upon it and that developing a commitment to learning as a lifelong activity should be a priority.

There are three main areas which you might want to consider:

- **Academic** – this would involve taking further courses (see section on developing yourself in higher levels of education above).

- **Professional/vocational** – which might include professional qualification and work-related training and development activities, normally sponsored by your employer (also discussed above).

- **Extra-mural/recreational activities** – which can include doing anything that you like, including participating in hobbies, sports, the arts, travel, etc. However, it is often the way in life that whatever you learn seems to come in useful somewhere along the way. Your current hobby might even become your next job!

A local employer told us...

The Chief Executive of a very successful medium-sized local company told us that he gladly paid for any of his staff to do whatever they wanted at evening class, not only because it made the staff happier but also because, in the end, it always seemed to prove useful to the company in some way.

We believe that all learning has the potential to provide new opportunities and new insights. It is all too easy to get so locked into a professional career that it makes the task of making work role transitions unnecessarily difficult (see also the above section on work role transitions). Looking outside of where you are – by developing new interests, knowledge or skills – helps you to locate where you are in the world and where you are going.

Having clear aims which you can both specify and articulate would seem to be a major determinant of good health and longevity. Having an idea of where you are going and why, not only seems to give people a goal in life but also a reason for being. How often do we hear stories of people achieving despite setbacks such as illness, disability or other misfortunes?

Throughout this book we have asked you to reflect upon aspects of yourself and your skills set. Learning about ourselves is potentially a lifelong activity and in

Chapter 2, when we looked at personal development planning, we made the point that the process is not just for higher education or just for employment, it is for life.

> ### Activity: Why stop now?
>
> Here are two questions to consider:
>
> - Why keep on growing?
> - Why stop growing now?

Lifelong learning is an element of what might be called personal growth and development. It takes place not only in education and employment but also in the sphere of private life beyond and there is no limit to what you might do – from climbing a mountain, through learning to play the piano, to embarking on a spiritual quest to know yourself more fully. Whatever you do will develop you in some respect and you will grow as a person.

Throughout this book we have asked you to first reflect upon your skills and then actively to develop them. Now that we are almost at the end of this book, it remains only for us to wish you good fortune in your journey through life. We know all too well that life's path can be rocky at times but also that developing good skills can help you at every stage in achieving your goals.

Follow-up activities

> ### TIME FOR ACTION – CHECKLIST
>
> Have you:
>
> - considered why you will need to continue developing yourself and upgrading your skills after your current course of studies?
> - thought about developing yourself further in higher levels of education?
> - examined how you could develop yourself within a professional career?
> - thought about how you might deal with work role transitions, unexpected changes of circumstances and how you could draw on your own transferable skills?
> - considered self-employment and entrepreneurship as an alternative to employment?
> - thought about developing your commitment to lifelong learning together with personal growth and development?

Further reading

Buckingham, M. and Clifton, D. O. (2005) *Now, Discover Your Strengths*. London: Simon & Schuster.

Cameron, S. (2008) *The MBA Handbook – Skills for Mastering Management*, 6th edition. Harlow: Pearson.

Churchill, H. and Sanders, T. (2007) *Getting Your PhD: A Practical Insiders Guide*. London: Sage Publications.

Cottrell, S. (2003) *Skills for Success: The Personal Development Planning Handbook*. Basingstoke: Palgrave Macmillan.

Jeffers, S. (1991) *Feel The Fear and Do it Anyway*. London: Arrow.

Moon, J. (1999) *Reflection in Learning and Professional Development*. London: Kogan Page.

O'Connor, J. (2002) *The NLP Workbook: A Practical Guide to Achieving Results you Want*. London: Element.

Websites to look up

- For information on careers and courses:

http://www.nusonline.co.uk/info/careers/
http://www.pcsexecutive.com/?gclid=CJKWz4C_pZICFQQF1Qod4la_RA

Time for review and reflection

This is your space to log your reflections on this chapter, to think about what you have learnt, how you will use it and what else you need to find out.

What were the key learning points of this chapter?

What are your strengths in the areas covered by this chapter?

What areas did you identify for development?

What have you learnt about yourself?

How will you use it?

What else do you need to learn or find out about in relation to this chapter?

References and Bibliography

Ambady, N. (1993) 'Half a Minute: Predicting Teacher Evaluations from Thin Slices of Non-verbal Behaviour and Physical Attractiveness,' *Journal of Personality and Social Psychology*, 64.

Ambady, N. and Rosenthal, R. (1992) 'Thin Slices of Expressive Behaviour as Predictors of Interpersonal Consequences: A Meta-analysis', *Psychological Bulletin*, Vol. 111: 256–274.

Aspey, L. (1998) *The Job Search Manual*, 2nd edition. Chalford: Management Books.

Baddeley, A. D. (1990) *Human Memory: Theory and Practice*. Hove: Lawrence Erlbaum Associates.

Bandler, R. and Grinder, J. (1976 and 1979), cited in O'Connor, J. and Seymour, F. (2002) *Introducing NPL: Psychological Skills for Understanding and Influencing People*. London: Element.

Belbin, M. (1993) *Team Roles at Work*. Oxford: Butterworth Heinemann.

Belbin, M. (2000) *Beyond the Team*. Oxford: Butterworth Heinemann.

Belbin Team Role Theory [online]. Available from: www.belbin.com/rte.asp?id8 [accessed: 18.03.08].

Bell, J. (2005) *Doing Your Research, A Guide for First-Time Researchers in Education, Health and Social Science,* 4th edition. Maidenhead: Open University Press.

Berne, E. (1968) *The Games People Play*. London: Penguin.

Berne, E. (1975) *What Do You Say After You Say Hello*? London: Corgi.

Billingham, J. (2003) *Giving Presentations*. Oxford: Oxford University Press.

Bird, J. and Pinch, C. (2002) *Autogenic Therapy*. Dublin: Newleaf.

Bloisi, W., Cook, C. W. and Hunsaker, P. L. (2007) *Management and Organisational Behaviour*, 2nd European edition. Maidenhead: McGraw-Hill Education.

Blumberg, B., Cooper, D. and Schindler, P. (2005) *Business Research Methods*. Maidenhead: McGraw-Hill.

Boud, D. (1986) *Implementing Student Self-Assessment*. New South Wales: Higher Education Research and Development Society of Australia.

Boyatzis, R. (2001) *How and Why Individuals Are Able to Develop Emotional Intelligence,* cited in Cherniss, C. and Goleman, D. (eds) (2001) *The Emotionally Intelligence Workplace*. San Francisco: Jossey-Bass.

Brain image [online]. Available from: http://www.science.ca/images/Brain_Witelson.jpg. [accessed: 27.03.08].

Buckingham, M. and Clifton, D. O. (2005) *Now, Discover Your Strengths*. London: Simon & Schuster.

Burns, T. and Sinfield, S. (2008) *Essential Study Skills: The Complete Guide to Success at University*, 2nd edition. London: Sage.

Buzan, T. (1974) *Use Your Head*. London: BBC Books.

Buzan, T. (1995) *The Mind Map Book*. London: BBC Books.

Byham, C. and Cox, J. (1988) *Zapp! The Lightning of Empowerment: How to Improve Productivity, Quality and Employee Satisfaction*. New York: Random House.

Cameron, S. (2008) *The Business Student's Handbook*, 4th edition. Harlow: Pearson.

Cameron, S. (2008) *The MBA Handbook – Skills for Mastering Management*, 6th edition. Harlow: Pearson.

CAPLITS Centre for Professional Literacies [online]. Available from: www.ioe.ac.uk/caplits/writingcentre/criticalreview.1tostart.htm [accessed 18.03.08].

Carr, A. (1995) *The Only Way to Stop Smoking Permanently*. London: Penguin Health Care and Fitness.

Cherniss, C. and Goleman, D. (eds) (2001) *The Emotionally Intelligent Workplace*. San Francisco: Jossey-Bass.

Chopra, D. (2001) *Perfect Health*. London: Bantam.

Churchill, H. and Sanders, T. (2007) *Getting Your PhD: A Practical Insiders Guide*. London: Sage Publications.

Cialdini, R. B. (2001) *Harnessing the Science of Persuasion*. Harvard Business Review, Oct.

Corfield, R. (1999) *How You Can Get the Job! Application Forms and Letters Made Easy*, 2nd edition. London: Kogan Page.

Corfield, R. (2007) *Preparing the Perfect CV: How to Make a Great Impression and Get the Job you Want*, 4th edition. London: Kogan Page.

Cornelius, N. (2001) *Human Resource Management: A Managerial Perspective*. London: Thomson Learning.

Cottrell, S. (1999) *The Study Skills Handbook*. Basingstoke: Palgrave Macmillan.

Cottrell, S. (2003) *Skills for Success: The Personal Development Planning Handbook*. Basingstoke: Palgrave Macmillan.

Cottrell, S. (2003) *The Study Skills Handbook*, 2nd edition. Basingstoke: Palgrave Macmillan.

Cottrell, S. (2005) *Critical Thinking Skills: Developing Effective Analysis and Argument*. Basingstoke: Palgrave Macmillan.

Cottrell, S. (2006) *The Exam Skills Handbook*. Basingstoke: Palgrave Macmillan.

Davidson, R. J. quoted in Goleman, D. (2003) *Destructive Emotions and How We Can Overcome Them*. London: Bloomsbury.

Davis, G. (1999) *Giving Feedback*. University of Brighton, School of Pharmacy *(Video Material)*.

Entwistle, N. J. and Marton, F. (1984) 'Changing conceptions of Learning and research', cited in Marton, F., Hounsell, D., Entwistle, N. J. (1984) *The Experience of Learning*. Edinburgh: Scottish Academic Press.

Feldman, R. (2000) *Power Learning, Strategies for Success in College and Life*. Maidenhead: McGraw-Hill Higher Education.

Goleman, D. (1998) *Working with Emotional Intelligence*. London: Bloomsbury Paperbacks.

Goleman, D. (2001) 'An EI-Based Theory of Performance' in Cherniss, C. and Goleman, D. (eds) *The Emotionally Intelligence Workplace*. San Francisco: Jossey-Bass.

Goleman, D. (2003) *Destructive Emotions and How We Can Overcome Them*. London: Bloomsbury.

Guirdham, M. (2002) *Interpersonal Skills at Work*, 3rd edition. Harlow: Pearson.

Hawkins, P. and Winter, J. (1995) *Skills for Graduates in the 21st Century*. Cambridge: Assoc. of Graduate Recruiters.

Herbert, I. and Rothwell, A. (2005) *Managing Your Placement: A Skills Based Approach*. Basingstoke: Palgrave.

Hill, G. W. (1982) 'Group Versus Individual Performance: Are N+1 Heads Better Than One?', *Psychological Bulletin, 91*.

Honey, P. (1994) *Learning Logs – A Way to Enhance Learning from Experience*. Maidenhead: Peter Honey Publications.

Honey, P. and Mumford, A. (1982) *The Manual of Learning Styles*. Maidenhead: Peter Honey Publications.

Hubel, D. H., Wiesel, T. N. and LeVay, S. (1977) *Plasticity of Ocular Dominance Columns in Monkey Striate Cortex*. Royal Society of London.

Huczynski, A. A. and Buchanan, D. A. (2007) *Organisational Behaviour – an Introductory Text*, 6th edition. Harlow: Pearson.

Hunsaker, P. L. (2005) *Management – A Skills Approach*, 2nd edition. Upper Saddle River, NJ: Pearson.

Jeffers, S. (1991) *Feel the Fear and Do it Anyway*. London: Arrow.

Kermani, K. (1996) *Autogenic Training*. London: Souvenir Press.

Kolb, D. A. (1984) *Experiential Learning: Experience as the Source of Learning and Development*. New Jersey: Prentice-Hall.

Kolb, D. A. and Fry, R. (1975) *Toward an Applied Theory of Experiential Learning*. New York: John Wiley & Sons.

Kuhn, T. S. (1970) *The Structure of Scientific Revolutions*. Chicago: University of Chicago Press.

Lee-Davies, L. (2007) *Developing Work and Study Skills*. London: Thomson.

Leonard, D. C. (1996) 'The Impact of Learning Goals on Self-directed Change in Educational and Management Development'. PhD thesis, Case Western Reserve University, UMI Dissertation Services.

Loehr, J. and Schwartz, T. (2003) *On Form*. London: Nicholas Brearley Publishing.

Malderez, A. and Bodoczky, C. (1999) *Mentor Courses: a resource book for trainer-trainers*. Cambridge: Cambridge Teacher Training and Development.

Marx, K. and Engels, F. (1967) *The Communist Manifesto*. Harmondsworth: Pelican Books.

Mayer, J. and Salovey, P. G. (1990) 'Emotional Intelligence', *Imagination, Cognition and Personality*, Vol. 9: 185–211.

Mehrabian, A. (1971) *Silent Messages*. Belmont, CA: Wadsworth.

Moon, J. (1999) *Reflection in Learning and Professional Development*. London: Kogan Page.

Moon, J. (2006) *Learning Journals: A Handbook of Reflective Practice and Professional Development*, 2nd edition. Abingdon: Routledge.

Mounsey, C. (2002) *Essays and Dissertations*. Oxford: Oxford University Press.

Mullins, L. J. (2007) *Management and Organisation Behaviour*, 8th edition. Harlow: Pearson.

O'Connor, J. (2002) *The NLP Workbook: A Practical Guide to Achieving the Results you Want*. London: Element.

O'Connor, J. and Seymour, F. (2002) *Introducing NPL: Psychological Skills for Understanding and Influencing People*, 3rd edition. London: Element.

O'Hara, S. (1998) *Studying at University and College*. London: Kogan Page.

Pease, A. (1984) *Body Language*. London: Sheldon Press.

Pedler, M. and Boydell, J. (1999) *Managing Yourself*. London: Lemos and Crane.

Perls, F. S. (1951) *Gestalt Therapy; Excitement and Growth in the Human Personality*. New York: Julian Press.

Pert, C. (1999) *Molecules of Emotion*. London: Pocket Books.

Pert, C. (2007) *Everything You Need To Know To Feel Good*. London: Hay House.

Peter Honey Publication [online]. Available from: www.peterhoney.com [accessed 18.03.2008].

Popper, K. R. (1989) *Conjectures and Refutations: the Growth of Scientific Knowledge*, 5th revised edition. London: Routledge.

Race, P. (1995) *Who Learns Wins*. London: Penguin.

Race, P. (2007) *How to Get a Good Degree: Making the Most of your Time at University*. Buckingham: Open University Press.

Ridley, D. (2008) *The Literature Review: A Step-by-Step Guide for Students*. London: Sage.

Russell, T. (1994) *Effective Feedback Skills*. London: Kogan Page.

Saunders, M., Thornhill, A. and Lewis, P. (2006) *Research Methods for Business Students,* 4th edition. London: FT/Prentice Hall.

Seeley, J. (2002) *Report Writing*. Oxford: Oxford University Press.

Smith, H. W. (1998) *The 10 Natural Laws of Time and Life Management*. London: Nicholas Brearley Publishing.

Smith, M. J. (1975) *When I Say No I feel Guilty*. New York: Bantam.

Spencer, L. and Spencer, S. (1993) *Competence at Work: Models for Superior Performance*. New York: John Wiley & Sons.

Stewart, I. and Joines, V. (1987) *TA Today*. Nottingham: Lifespace.

Tannenbaum, R. and Schmidt, W. H. (1973) 'How To Choose a Leadership Pattern', *Harvard Business Review,* May–June: 162–75 and 178–80, cited in Mullins, L. J. (2007) *Management and Organisation Behaviour*, 8th edition. Harlow: Pearson.

Topping, K. J., Smith, E. F., Swanson, I. and Elliot, A. (2000) 'Formative Peer Assessment Between Postgraduate Students', *Assessment and Evaluation in Higher Education*, Vol. 24, No. 2.

Tuckman, B. W. and Jensen, M. C. (1977) 'Stages of Small Group Development', *Group and Organisational Studies,* Vol. 2, No. 3: 419–27, cited in Mullins, L.J. (2007) *Management and Organisation Behaviour*, 8th edition. Harlow: Pearson.

Walliman, N. (2004) *The Undergraduate Dissertation: The Essential Guide for Success*. London: Sage.

Woodruffe, C. (2000) *Development and Assessment Centres*, 3rd edition. London: CIPD.

Index

absenteeism 83
academic rigour 133
academic writing 148–9
action words 122, 189
active experimentation 107
active listening 47, 228
active verbs 212, 215
adjustment to living independently 76
adult response, transactional analysis 51
affirmations 19, 174
alcohol 96–8
amygdala takeovers 20–1
antithesis 116, 117
anxiety 88, 174–5, 184
appendices, reports 160
application process
  active verbs, using 212
  cover letters 218–20
  curriculum vitae, developing see CV
    (curriculum vitae)
  developing content for 211–14
  failure to become shortlisted 220
  planning application form 214–15
  STAR technique, using 212–14, 215
  upgrading of skills 209–11
aptitude tests, assessment centres 233
assertiveness 61–3
assessment
  degree classifications 120–1
  formative 120
  peer 123, 163
  presence 15
  reasons for 120
  self-assessment 123, 160–2
  summative 120
  tutor 123, 163
  understanding assessments 121–3
assessment centre
  activities 232–3
  defined 231

assessment centre *cont.*
  effective performance at 231–3
  failure to become shortlisted 220
attention spans 186
audio-visual aids 172
autogenic training 90
autonomic nervous system 118
autonomy 56–7

Baddeley, A. D. 69
Bandler, R. 36
Belbin, M. 125
Berlin School of writers 112
Berne, Eric 50, 51, 55, 57
blaming 90
body language 57–9, 172, 226
bookshops 16
boutons 118
Boyatzis, R. 29
brain 118
brainstorming 119, 169
breathing exercises 89
broken record, assertiveness technique 63
budgets 78–9
burn out 182
Buzan, T. 119

can do thinking 182, 184
cardiovascular exercise 95
careers office, university 201
Carr, A. 97
child response, transactional analysis 51
closed/directional questions 46
coding 142
comfort zone 38
communications
  see also feedback; interpersonal skills;
    people skills
  face-to-face 65
  non-verbal 57–9, 172, 226